The Massawippi Monster
and
Other Friends of Mine

For Marion and Jimmy,

Best wishes on your 50th
Wedding Anniversary

Ronald Sutherland

Acknowledgements

Many of these short pieces have appeared in the *Montreal Gazette, London Free Press* and *Cleveland Plain Dealer*. A few have appeared in the *Winnipeg Free Press, Wichita Eagle Beacon, Toronto Globe and Mail, Baltimore Sun* and *Saint John Telegraph-Journal*. "Muskrats and Maple Syrup" has been reprinted in the Canadian edition of the **Lado English Series**. "Does Remembrance Day Make Sense?" has been reprinted in both the English and French Canadian editions of *Reader's Digest*, "Bilingual Belts and Buckles" was used in a training manual for the RCMP, and "The Monster of Lake Massawippi" was included in the anthology edited by J.R. Colombo, *Extraordinary Experiences*.

I wish to thank my long-time colleague and friend, Cormac Gerard Cappon for his proof-reading expertise, Suzanne O'Connor for her advice and unwavering encouragement, and my publishers Frank Tierney and Glenn Clever for their efforts on my behalf and that of many other Canadian authors.

The Massawippi Monster
and
Other Friends of Mine

Ronald Sutherland

Borealis Press
Ottawa, Canada
2004

*We acknowledge the financial assistance of the
Government of Canada through the Book Publishing Industry
Development Program (BPIDP) for our publishing activities.*

Canada

National Library of Canada Cataloguing in Publication Data
Sutherland, Ronald, 1933-
    The Massawippi Monster and other friends of mine /
Ronald Sutherland

ISBN 0-88887-203-8

    1. Sutherland, Ronald, 1933—Anecdotes. 2. Authors,
Canadian (English) — 20th centure—Biography. I. Title.

PS8587.U8Z53 2004   C818'.5403   C2003-907016-6

Cover design by Bull's Eye Design, Ottawa

Printed and bound in Canada on acid-free paper.

IN MEMORIAM

For Velma Jean Carter Sutherland,
A woman or rare beauty, insight and artistic skills,
wife and mother dearly loved by
Janet, Kate, Velman, Winona, Colin
and husband Ron.
She lives on in these pages.

Table of Contents

Preface

While I was compiling this selection of my more
humorous and whimsical vignettes, then placing them
in more or less chronological order, it occurred to me
that what I have been writing for various newspapers
over the last few years, however unintentionally and
haphazardly, is a kind of autobiography. I have
described my childhood in the East End of Montreal,
the adventures and misadventures of my youth and
college years, my wife and five children, my family
and in-laws, my grandson, my dog and my cats. On the
other hand, this conglomeration is really quite different
from proper autobiographies, which are generally
serious and generally do not tell the whole truth.

Proper autobiographies, I imagine, are written
because of some compulsion to justify one's existence, and I have never felt the need to justify mine. I
was born through no fault of my own in the front room
of a cold-water flat at 4478 Adam Street, during a
severe blizzard on the evening of November 10th,
1933, and since then I have simply plodded along and
avoided blizzards as best I could. For a while I was
able to put everything I owned into a medium-sized
suitcase and two cardboard boxes. Then one day I
found myself married, and the next day, it seems, I had
a houseful of kids, animals, books and other necessi-
ties of life which only a fleet of eighteen-wheelers
could transport. And I have a feeling that the short
pieces in this collection are in essence feeble attempts
to explain to myself what happened.

When I began writing these vignettes, my inten-
tion was to provide light-hearted antidotes to the

depressing news of disasters and calamities of every sort filling the dailies. Since then the news seems only to have gotten steadily worse, and it is perhaps an appropriate time to increase the dosage of antidote.

Special Occasions, People and Creatures

The Monster of Lake Massawippi

It was a little past midnight as I paddled my canoe across Lake Massawippi in the hills of southern Quebec near the Vermont border. The water was still quite calm, but the increasingly loud rumblings and flashes of lightning in the distance indicated that a storm was closing in fast. Every few minutes the moon emerged from behind the clouds to pour shimmering white light over the waves. The effect was eerie, almost otherworldly. Taking my eyes off the yellow porch lamp on the far shore which was serving as my guide beacon, I stopped paddling for a moment to survey the autumn night and the lake, gloriously silent now that the motor boats were all tied to their docks.

Then I heard a splash . . . and a hissing sound, like some creature drawing breath. I turned, and what I saw literally took away my breath. The moonlight glared from two greenish eyes and from huge, hideous, protruding fangs. Curving upward snakelike to twin points, the head was a foot or so out of the water. and it was definitely coming towards me, bobbing slightly up and down.

I admit that I froze in panic, gripping my paddle with both hands, and in the next few seconds all the stories I had dismissed with a wink and a chuckle came thundering back into my mind.

An old man in a bar, shortly after I settled by Lake Massawippi, told me how he had once hooked a large sturgeon, at least six feet long originally. After playing the fish for two hours, suddenly he was able to haul it in without a struggle. Then he discovered

2

that the sturgeon had been bitten in half. "Sliced clean right across in one bite. Now what yuh figure could do that?" he asked, staring into his beer and breaking a pickled egg in two to emphasize his point.

A woman I know who types university theses rented a house up the lake one summer. Conscientious and hard-headed, Paulette used to get up at five a.m. and work on the front veranda of her cottage. One morning, just as she was lining up a page in the typewriter, a movement on the lake caught her eye. She looked out to see, in her own words, "a fin about a foot and a half out of the water, tearing across the lake at a terrific speed, leaving a wake like an ocean liner."

The moon slipped behind the clouds again, plunging me into pitch darkness. The frightful hissing grew louder and quicker, and I could actually feel hot breath on my arms, but I still could not force myself to paddle and at least try to escape.

Oddly enough, a few days earlier, my wife and I had gone out for a midnight canoe ride and had tipped the canoe. She can't swim but was wearing a life belt, so we simply held on for an hour or so, cheering each other as we kicked our feet and stroked with one arm, and eventually we managed to propel the boat to shore.

My God, I thought, the breath growing hotter on my frozen arms, what if we had known that there was really a monster in the lake? How could we have kept our presence of mind?

They're in Loch Ness for sure. Why not Massawippi? Plumb lines, I had once heard, have never reached the murky bottom of some parts of the lake. Great caves are down there, and quite probably an underground channel connecting with vast Lake Memphremagog, which is shared by Canada and the United States. The creature might even be American. The adjoining state of Vermont is apparently full of leaky nuclear plants, which can cause horrible mutations I'm told—in other words, monsters.

Just this summer a panel of 200 scientists met in Shelburne, Vermont, to study the photographs, sonar readings and 144 sightings over 400 years—explorer Samuel de Champlain saw a "large, snakelike beast" in 1609—of "Champ," the monster of Lake Champlain. Dr. George Zug, chairman of the Smithsonian Institute's Department of Vertebrate Zoology, summed up the panel's findings by saying, "There's at least a population of large animals of some kind."

Serious scientists they were, 200 of them.

That guy who disappeared two years ago. They said that he was having an affair with a young thing and wanted to get away from his unsympathetic wife.

They'll no doubt say the same thing about me when no trace of my body can be found. The gossips will have a field day for sure . . . I knew my wife couldn't swim . . .tried to get rid of her a few nights earlier by tipping the canoe, but it didn't work. So I faked a disappearance. Always was a dubious character. Oddball friends. Weird habits. Too many kids. Obscure books. Scruffy clothes. Kept bees up on the hill.

Just a matter of seconds now. The moonlight is spreading across the lake again. The storm is veering to the south. And as I stare transfixed towards the head in the water, resigned now to go to my fate like a blubbering zombie, suddenly the head barks at me.

A familiar bark. A familiar old yellow mutt.

I'll never know why my dog took a notion to swim out to the canoe. He loves the water, and all summer he has been trying to catch water skiers. But in the middle of the night with a storm brewing?

And in a lake full of monsters?

Bilingual Belts and Buckles

Although not surprising and perhaps even psychologically necessary at the moment, it is saddening to find out that Canada is becoming increasingly unilingual. According to a report by Richard Joy, expert on linguistic geography and author of a perceptive book on the subject, *Languages in Conflict*, Quebec is becoming more exclusively francophone, English Canada is becoming more exclusively anglophone, and from north-eastern Ontario to northern New Brunswick runs a bilingual belt where the two languages buckle together.

What is good about this phenomenon is that it is permitting the Québécois at long last to build the cultural security they need if they are to function in the nation as equals. The process, of course, was gathering force long before Bill 101, which was the rasp to get rid of the rough edges.

What is sad is that for a time at least, and especially for those of us who are bilingual, much of the variety and amusement will be missing from Canadian life. For when two languages are being used side by side, many funny things do happen.

Like the experience of a Toronto lady I know who went to a party in Chicoutimi and became almost desperate wondering what she had to do to get a drink. Whenever she was offered one, she smiled appreciatively and said *merci*—but then the hostess just smiled too and walked away, and did not come back with a drink.

Since the dialogues the lady had studied in her high-school French course had not included cocktail parties and the like, she did not know that when you are offered something in French, saying *merci* is the equivalent of saying *non merci* or "No thank you." If your need is great, then you say *oui* or *s'il vous plaît* or *ben sûr* or "okay," or else you go and get what you want, which is perhaps the most effective course to follow.

Common pitfalls of linguistic co-existence are the *faux amis* or false friends, words which look the same in English and French but which have quite different meanings. An English-speaking clergyman was once led into temptation by the French verb *blesser*, meaning "to hurt" or "to do harm to," and shocked half of an ecumenical congregation by rendering "God bless you" as *Que Dieu vous blesse*.

Québécois get fooled too. The word *actuellement* in French, for instance, means "now" or "at present" and not "actually," as a francophone might expect. It is always entertaining to hear government officials and other people of consequence make remarks such as "The whole province has been blacked out by a power failure, but actually there is nothing wrong," or "He served the community selflessly for many years, and actually he is dead."

Words for the citizens of nations are highly irregular in English—an Englishman, a Frenchman, but an American, an Italian, and so on. Yet despite the irregularity, it is still a bit startling to hear, as I did a while ago, a woman tell me that her sister is married to "an English," or to have a person from a central European country referred to as a "Poleman."

When languages are concerned, what would appear to be reasonable cannot always be trusted. On the menu of an elegant restaurant I once saw "pineapple" translated, quite reasonably, as *pommes de pin*. The problem is that "pineapple" is *ananas* in French, while *pommes de pin* are "pine cones," which are not too appetizing, even if served with fresh dairy cream.

Dictionaries cannot always be trusted either. There was once a cow-crossing sign on Route 143 in Stanstead County in Quebec which read *Traverse des Vaches* in French, but apparently the farmer went to an old dictionary to get the English, which read "Seapassage of Cows."

A recent ad for shoes in a newspaper announced, "Not all styles available in every store." Now the French for "style" is genre, but there is another word dangerously close to it, gendre, and that is the word which got into the French version of the ad: *Pas tous les gendres dans chaque magasin*. Since *gendre* means "son-in-law," francophone customers were thus informed that all the sons-in-law were not in each store, which in a way, I suppose, was reassuring.

Bilingual labels on commercial products have led to a few howlers and much amusement for bilingual shoppers. One spot-remover on the market directs users to rub in the liquid for ten seconds in English. French spots, however, would appear to be much harder to remove, for francophone users are told to rub it in for ten minutes.

People who are bilingual, to be sure, are the ones who can most fully appreciate the humour, the diversity and richness of life in Canada, at least for the time being and in Mr. Joy's bilingual belt.

There is a story told of a unilingual anglophone who applied for a job in Quebec City in the old days before Bill 101. When the personnel manager turned him down, he got angry.

"I speak one of the official languages of Canada," shouted the job-seeker, "and I demand to be treated accordingly."

"Of course," said the personnel manager, "but let me tell you about the cat that chased the mouse, and the mouse ran into a hole. The cat waited beside the hole, twitching its tail the way cats do. But that little mouse was a smart mouse, and he stayed in the hole.

"So after about two hours, the cat got up, backed away a few inches and went WOOF WOOF. Ah, the dog has come and chased away the cat, thought the mouse, and he came out of the hole.

"The cat pounced on the mouse and ate it up. And while he was cleaning his whiskers with his paws, he was saying to himself, 'It sure pays to be bilingual.'"

I have a strong hunch that no matter what happens to the various segments and belts of Canada, it will always pay to be bilingual. Besides, it's a lot of fun.

Roll Out the Barrel

Like most other Canadians probably, I am out in the cold when it comes to knowing exactly what the nation's position is with respect to energy resources. One morning I pick up a newspaper and learn that Canada's petroleum reserves are sufficient to cancel a thousand winters, then the following day I read a magazine article explaining in cold detail that the oil wells of Alberta will be going the way of the buffalo herds in about ten years or so.

What I do know with certainty, however, is that besides the Arabs and the oil companies, one other group is reaping profits from the current energy demands—the junk dealers in the Eastern Townships of Quebec. Mind you, to the outsider junk dealers do not always present themselves as junk dealers. They buy junk, to be sure, but they sell antiques, and the Townships region is famous for its many antique dealers and huge annual antique shows.

I had occasion to stop by a junk dealer the other day, a man called Danny or Daniel, depending on whether one thinks of him as English or French. There is no way to tell from speaking to him. And I doubt if he knows himself, or even cares, which is his proper language group and whether there is anything distinct about his society. A politician's despair, Danny-Daniel. A threat to the whole issue of national issues, and a scheming profiteer besides.

Anyway, I stopped by his junk yard to see about buying a Quebec heater–type, pot-bellied stove. My house, of course, has a modern oil furnace. Beautiful it is, with fibreglass air filters, atomizer for the humidity, remote wall thermostat and all the rest.

I remember spending the winter in northern England once, where I rented a house heated with two fireplaces. How romantic, I and my family thought. We had always fancied a fireplace, and suddenly we had two of them.

But the house was in what was called a "smoke-less zone," which means that instead of wood or coal, a specially manufactured fuel has to be burned. That winter was the coldest the British Isles had experienced for 75 years, freezing over the ponds and cracking the sewer pipes across the land. I soon discovered that getting the special fuel burning was like trying to light stones.

I was equally unsuccessful with British Railways, which somehow for three weeks, on a siding in Edinburgh I later learned, lost the two trunks containing all the winter clothing of my wife, my five children and myself.

Most men with half a hormone dream of beautiful women, I suppose, luscious creatures clad in sheer negligées holding bunches of grapes and beckoning them into cushioned boudoirs. Generally I dream along those lines too, on a good night. But during those long, frosty, damp, bone-chilling nights in England, by God, I dreamed about thermostats! I would be casually strolling by the thermostat on the wall. Then I would take a notion to set it at 72, maybe even 73 or 73 and a half. But as I reached up to turn the control, the wretched thing would fade away, just like those gorgeous girls in dreams when you make a grab for them. And I'd wake up to find that I was loosening the top of the hot water bottle, and the water was pouring into the bed.

It will be understood, then, why I worry about

heating my house and why, after hearing so much about rising fuel costs, I decided to look for a Quebec heater, one of those pudgy little stoves of my childhood which burns wood, coal, old furniture, shoes or anything else available.

"Sure," said Danny-Daniel, "got jist what yer lookin' fer."

Then he showed me what surely must have been the original. It was rusted through in several places. The doors were hanging off. A couple of the knobs you turn to shake down the ashes were missing. "Wouldn't take much to fix 'er up," said he cheerfully. "Already sold all the others. A lot of Americans come up this way and take back whatever they can."

"How much?" I asked.

"Seventy-five dollars," he said.

"You're out of your mind," I said. "Give you five bucks."

"Nossir," he said, "fifty and that's it. I kin sell 'er to a Yank this afternoon, maybe tomorrow, Saturday fer sure. I got a wife an' kids to feed, yuh know."

"Yeah, me too," I said and turned to leave.

"Hey, why don't yuh make yerself a stove outa an oil drum," he said. "That's what a lot of 'em are doing."

"Is that right?"

"Sure," he said, "nothin' to it. I kin let yuh have an old oil drum fer a couple a ten spots."

Well, finally I decided to put my faith in Alberta. If the oil people out there can't send any oil, then maybe we can talk them into at least sending the empty oil drums to Quebec.

Muskrats and Maple Syrup

They're seeing flying saucers again in the Eastern Townships of Quebec. One couple has applied for a government grant to investigate what they claim is a UFO base near Owl's Head, just east of Lake Memphremagog, and a man by the name of Pierre Côté has witnessed what he calls *"une tache brillante"*—a brilliant spot—travel from north to south over the southwest horizon.

Mr. Côté, who is from the town of Victoriaville, says the flattened luminous ball was moving both up and down as well as from side to side as it followed its course. One would almost think that it was looking for something, or perhaps—and here the thought becomes a bit ominous—doing something.

Certainly there have been some mysterious forces operating lately in the Townships. Consider the maple trees, for example. Now as any envious Vermonter will tell you, or should at least have the common decency to admit, the Townships area has the world's best maple products: clear, golden-hued syrup, sugar, toffee, and what is known as *sucre mou*, a kind of maple butter which is irresistibly delicious spread on toast or on a piece of homemade bread. A thick slice of bread with maple butter is like a full-course meal, packed with vitamins, minerals and enough calories, I'm sure, to sabotage a weight-watchers' club for a month. But it's so good.

Anyway, as everybody knows, maple syrup is made in the spring, March and April, when a combination of warm sunny days and cold nights causes the sap to run. It's the right time of the year, too, before the planting season and after the farmers have finished their winter wood-cutting, when there is plenty of fuel to keep the big, flat sap pans at a boil. But this year, alarmingly, the sap has been running in January, the middle of the winter. That's not supposed to happen. One man involved in maple products for years, Mr. Gérard Boissonault, has even been tapping his trees, and he says that the sap is running as in the full bloom of spring. There have been two big flows already, he claims, and he has the syrup to prove it. In more than a quarter century that he has been making maple syrup, Mr. Boissonault has never seen the like.

Could it have anything to do with Mr. Côté's flying saucer? You never know. And another strange phenomenon has been noted by Mr. Boissonault, who maintains a kind of game preserve on his land. For a long time now he has been observing the habits of wildlife, and he claims that the weather can be predicted by the actions of some of the animals. He doesn't mention raccoons, called *ratons laveurs*— little washer rats—in Quebec, and I'm personally very glad about that, because I don't trust raccoons. You could put your garbage in a bank vault and the raccoons would still figure out a way to get at it and spread it out over a square mile.

Mr. Boissonault's weather predictions are based instead on muskrats, which he believes are highly trustworthy. Apparently the muskrats have been building their nests much higher than usual this year, which means that high water and extensive flooding are indicated for the spring. Yet there is hardly anything to cause a flood. Because of all the warm weather we've been having, there is not much snow around, about 25 inches less than normal. Or if you prefer, about 63.5 centimetres less than normal.

From a strictly mathematical point of view, I suppose, the metric system makes some sense, especially for people who have a notion of where to put decimal points. But in a vast and cold country like Canada, it is psychologically wrong. It gives the impression that distances are longer.

We had been accustomed, for instance, to driving a stretch of only 95 miles from Sherbrooke to Montreal, then suddenly the trip was lengthened to 152 kilometres. There was a time, also, when during a good part of the winter the temperature was a positive, above-zero degrees Fahrenheit—maybe five or seven or ten—and we all knew that the weather was fine. We began to dig out the long-johns and earmuffs only when the temperature was negative, minus something or other. Now the temperature is always minus—even a balmy 30 degrees Fahrenheit is –1.1 Celsius. The whole winter is negative these days. And even when we have less snow than normal, it seems like more.

This year, says Mr. Boissonault, even the metric system cannot disguise the fact that we haven't been getting as much snow as usual—so far, that is. The ski resort people can't even cry in their *après-ski* beer, because there is no skiing to be *après*. But the muskrats are never wrong, swears Mr. Boissonault, so something drastic is bound to happen. Six feet of snow on the 24th of May perhaps. Or maybe the raccoons have been briefing the muskrats on how to mess up peoples' lives. Then there is Mr. Côté's flying saucer. Maybe it's having an effect on the muskrats or the weather, or both. And I'm willing to bet that the flying saucer operates on the metric system.

It all makes me think of what the American writer and naturalist Henry David Thoreau wrote in his famous book *Walden*: "The life in us is like the water in the river. It may rise this year higher than man has ever known it, and flood the parched uplands; even this may be the eventful year, which will drown all our muskrats."

Well, we in the Eastern Townships of Quebec can at least take comfort in one thing—our muskrats are ready for it.

Country Closed Until Further Notice

Astronomical figures, I used to think, aside from their pertinence to the actual science of astronomy, could also be useful to describe the population of China, the salaries of basketball players or the export profits of Japan. But they could never be applied to anything in Canada.

From a report out of Calgary, Alberta, however, I have learned that the Canadian Petroleum Association estimates that 260 billion dollars will be needed for exploration, development and operating expenses if the country is to achieve self-sufficiency in oil production in the foreseeable future. That's right—$260,000,000,000! And at the present rate of inflation, which has joined death and taxes as one of the inevitables of this worldly existence, a few more zeros can probably be added.

It boggles the mind. In fact, like the distances to the galaxies, it is quite beyond human comprehension. In simpler if not less awesome terms perhaps, the estimated amount required comes to some $10,000 for every Canadian man, woman and child, or about $50,000 per family.

The only hope for any reasonable person who does not own shares in an oil company is that somehow after all these years, God in his mercy, however less infinite than petro-dollars, will finally grant Canada a government, and that that government will refuse to spend the money as currently projected by the Canadian Petroleum Association.

From the standpoint of the general public, it is difficult to imagine a more monumental example of

throwing good money after bad. We know that petroleum is a non-renewable resource. We know what
happens when supplies run short or when the big
companies and the OPEC nations see the chance for
an extra barrel of bucks. We have also helplessly
witnessed the result when one of those two-football-
field-sized tankers breaks in half off some coastline,
even when the captain is dead sober.

Two hundred and sixty billion dollars! What fraction of that amount would it take to perfect and
institute partial solar heating for Canadian homes,
tidal energy in the Bay of Fundy with its 70-foot
flows, gasohol for many of our machines, wind
power, effective electric cars and mass-transit
systems, and God knows what other dependable,
renewable, Canadian-owned alternatives?

But I suppose that is really too much to hope for,
too much like common sense, too far removed from
the concerns of the job-creating giants like General
Motors and Standard Oil. Fortunately, however,
another practical alternative suggests itself.

Simply close down the country each winter.

With $50,000 per family, say $10,000 a year for
an initial period of five years, it will be possible to
form a consortium of travel agents to arrange for the
entire Canadian population to go to reasonable resorts
in the southern U.S., Mexico and the Caribbean
during those energy-wasteful winter months. We will
all loll in the sunshine, swim and snorkel, sip cheap
rum punch, get to know one another at last, listen
with glee to the continental weather broadcasts and
trade stories of blizzards long ago and far away.

The current problems of national unity and
Quebec as a distinct society will simply vanish from

our lives like the sleet and freezing rain. It is a well-known fact that once out of the country, Canadians, whether francophone, anglophone or allophone, suddenly discover that they are very much alike. Even in the so-called mother countries of Great Britain and France, Canadians find that they have more in common with each other than with their more or less co-linguists, *les Français de France* or the British English. It's a matter, I suppose, of a whole complex of shared history and values, which we are reluctant or afraid to acknowledge when we're at home. Or perhaps it's simply that we have to leave it for a while before we realize that we actually do have a country, and a relatively good one at that.

Each year the Great Exodus will take place on Christmas Eve with singing and dancing and the sound of trumpets. The Governor-General, in a Panama hat and Bermuda shorts, under a plastic overcoat if necessary, will be telecast from coast to coast slapping a padlock on the Houses of Parliament. This exhibition, of course, will be largely symbolic, since it is understood that our elected representatives would be heading south in any case, but it would serve to inspire the masses and smother any possible dissension among skiers, trappers and masochists.

Then, as the legendary John Diefenbaker would have put it, 30 million or so Canadians will be on the move. A vast cavalcade of buses, cars, bicycles, tricycles, roller blades, Red River carts, calèches, wheelbarrows and Volkswagen vans crossing the border in peace and good will, horns blaring and bells jingling and children screaming, to be welcomed with open hands.

Pulled off annually by Canadians, this event will in fact be comparable to various great mass movements in history, like the gold rush of 1849, or the sweep of Attila the Hun's hordes across Europe, or the retreat of Napoleon's armies from Russia. The supplemental benefits, apart from nice suntans, will be almost impossible to calculate—more astronomical numbers of dollars in fuel oil, snow removal costs, sand, salt, snow tires, cough medicine, antifreeze and 20-percent wool underwear and socks.

The money saved, over and above the $260 billion already mentioned, would no doubt be sufficient to allow the total population to continue wintering in the South indefinitely, or at least until the "Greenhouse Effect" finally converts the Alberta tar sands into tropical rain forest. And we are assured by environmentalists that many of our leading industrialists, with government co-operation and in conjunction with other industrialists around the world, are earnestly working on that now.

Frontier Frolics

In French they call the border *la frontière*, and considering what goes on daily along the thousands of miles of so-called undefended boundary line between Canada and the United States, the term frontier may be entirely appropriate.

It's a kind of no-man's land, an area where the usual rules of behaviour do not apply and which brings out the lust for adventure, even the primitive, in human beings. People who normally live quiet, conventional lives can be turned into scheming desperadoes when trying to slip southward across the line with a few antiques, a couple of Cuban cigars and tickets for tax-free Loto prizes, or northward with a carton of cigarettes or a bottle or two for a festive occasion. And they can be transformed into pitiful, sputtering dolts when they get caught and have to watch the customs officers, shockingly immune to the spirit of decency and international good will, confiscate the Loto tickets or pour the booze down the drain.

One would have thought that the difference between the Canadian and American dollar in recent years would be enough to cool the smuggling urge of Canadians at least, but apparently not. For one thing, the Americans in bordering states, with typical Yankee ingenuity, sometimes accept Canadian money at par, a move calculated to drive their northern neighbours into a buying frenzy which more than offsets any loss on the part of the merchant. Besides, inflation in Canada seems to have created a wide divergence in the prices of everything from

21

Christmas decorations to kitchen gadgets, especially in a state like New Hampshire, which diabolically aggravates the situation by having no sales tax at all and by selling half-gallons of vodka for under $10.

The people of neighbouring Quebec, which also shares boundaries with Maine, Vermont and New York, have had centuries of practice in dealing with the American border. Smuggling is something of a regional sport, complete with rules, prizes and penalties.

There's the story, for instance, of the director of a small stage troupe which was invited to perform in Vermont. He had a van to transport the props, including a large cardboard box painted to look like a television set. Well, he went to Vermont, taking his wife and little boy along for the trip, and on the way back he was asked the usual question:

"Anything to declare, sir?"

"Nothing at all," replied the director cheerfully, explaining the strictly cultural purpose of the excursion. Then he added with a slightly nervous laugh, "Of course, we've got that beautiful colour TV over there," pointing to the cardboard stage prop. Both he and his wife joined the customs officer in a good chuckle over that one, and they were just about to pull away when the stage director's son got into the act with an unrehearsed line.

"You should see the nice new colour TV Daddy put underneath the box," piped up the child.

Altogether a bad scene, one might say. Never trust a mouthy brat—that's one of the cardinal rules of frontier frolics. Another rule is never to annoy customs officials to even the slightest degree. Their vision seems decidedly to improve with irritation.

I knew a girl once with the simple name of Ann Smith. Now in many ways it is good to have a common name—people tend to spell it and pronounce it correctly, especially at motel registration counters. But it doesn't do to have too common a name when crossing a border. Shortly before reunification, a Welsh miners' choir was held up six hours before being allowed into East Germany to give a concert. Three-quarters of the singers were named Jones; the border guards were sure it was a capitalist plot.

Ann Smith, poor soul, from the Isle of Lewis, Scotland, always had trouble. Then the ultimate occurred when a hometown friend, who by some wicked twist of fate and family was also called Ann Smith, came to stay with her, and the two girls decided to visit a friend in Boston.

"Name?" the border officer asked the first girl.

"Ann Smith."

"Where were you born?"

"Isle of Lewis, Scotland."

Then he turned immediately to the other girl. "What's your name?"

"Ann Smith."

The officer raised an eyebrow. Wheels were obviously beginning to turn in his head. "Where were you born?" he continued.

"Isle of Lewis, Scotland."

By a stroke of luck the girls had gotten a friendly official in a good mood. They were both pretty, and I suppose that helps. In any event, instead of ordering them to the dreaded inner office, he just smiled and said:

"Oh, so you're sisters then."

And that is when the first Ann, a little too quick-witted for her own good perhaps, made her mistake. "Yes sir," she replied. "Our mother was daft. She had nine daughters, and she named every one of us Ann."

"Inside!" shouted the border man. The girls were there for hours.

Despite minor setbacks from time to time, however, the frontier sport continues, reaching world series intensity at the height of the summer tourist season or when Christmas shopping is upon us. Many were led to believe that with the adoption of the Free Trade Agreement (FTA) between Canada and the United States, there would be unrestricted movement of goods across the border, only to discover that the FTA does not apply to ordinary people but to large corporations in the export business. In other words, apart from branch plants of American companies being closed in Canada and various small enterprises being lured south of the border by lower taxes and wages, nothing much has changed, especially for the cross-border traveller.

Which is probably just as well. In fact, Canada and the United States act as safety-valves for each other. Besides, who would want to spoil the sport which the good citizens of both countries have practised with skill for so many years, and which affords them such challenge and entertainment?

Country Doctor

How a man once performed a successful lobotomy on himself was one of Dr. Hector MacDougall's favourite and most bizarre stories. The man, as I recall, was being treated for the incapacity to control violent, often psychopathic behaviour, at the Bellevue Hospital of the TV series "Barney Miller" fame.

Dr. MacDougall was on emergency-room duty at the time in a large downtown New York City hospital, and the psychiatric patient in question had somehow managed to drive a nail into his own forehead. The claw hammer he had used was still lying on the stretcher beside him as he was rushed into the operating room.

"How on earth can we get that nail out?" asked the assisting intern.

"Pass me the hammer," said MacDougall.

The indelicate operation was a success, the man soon recovered from his head injury, and according to Dr. MacDougall, follow-up reports from Bellevue announced that he no longer suffered from uncontrollable violence. However inadvertently, he had cured himself.

Country doctors are apparently a disappearing species these days. Medical men and women quite understandably like to stay close to the large urban centres with sophisticated facilities, and when they venture into rural areas, generally it is to vacation at their summer cottages or to check out their beef herds and other investments.

The tiny village of North Hatley, however, located on Lake Massawippi in the Eastern

25

Townships of Quebec, has been singularly blessed. We have a town doctor now, and for many years until his death four years ago, we had the services of the legendary Dr. Hector MacDougall.

He was a brilliant diagnostician and a surgeon of wide and varied experience before he became a country doctor. He had worked alongside physicians such as the famous American surgeon Dr. Michael DeBakey, and he had practised in Montreal and the Caribbean as well as in New York. He was also a compulsive and gifted raconteur.

He could, in fact, by means of his stories alone, raise or lower my blood pressure by several notches. And if there was something he couldn't cure, he always found a way to make it a lot easier to live with the affliction. For example, a few years ago I developed a kind of fingernail rot, probably caused by some fungus picked up in the Caribbean. Convinced that my fingers were going to fall off, I made an appointment with Hector and held up my hands nervously.

He took one look at them and smiled. Then he held out his own hands, and for the first time I noticed that some of his fingernails were mangled in the same way as my own. "They've been that way for 35 years," he said as he leaned forward to examine my hands.

"Forget it," I replied. "Your waiting room is packed."

Another time when Hector was on emergency-room duty in a New York hospital, a man was brought in severely cut up from a knife attack. As Hector worked desperately to stitch the victim together again, the man kept urging him to hurry up. "What's the hurry? You're not going anywhere," Hector told him.

"I'm gonna get that s.o.b.," the patient replied. Then he jumped off the operating table, grabbed a scalpel and bolted out the door.

"And sure enough," Hector said, "a half hour later they wheeled in another guy more carved up than the first one. I had to wonder if it all made sense."

In a way Dr. Hector MacDougall had the ideal personality for a rural GP, but in another way perhaps he didn't. He was a highly sensitive, compassionate man, and as a result he loaded himself with the pains and anxieties of all of his patients.

He was also greatly concerned about the mindless violence in the world, an attitude no doubt exacerbated in emergency rooms. If he were still alive today, he would be despairing about the way violence seems to be ever increasing—in the big cities, in Bosnia, Nigeria, the Middle East, everywhere.

Man's capacity to maim and kill is clearly outstripping even the capabilities of gifted doctors like Hector MacDougall to cure and keep people alive. Maybe the only solution is to issue every human being with a hammer and a handful of nails.

Does Remembrance Day Make Sense?

Whatever their distinctions, the towns and hamlets across Canada generally have one common feature— a small park with a flowerbed and a brass plaque or a stone tablet listing the names of local people who fell in the wars.

Once a year a ceremony takes place in the park. Wreaths are laid, prayers are intoned by clergymen of the various denominations, and a bugler plays Last Post. If a bugler is not available, as is increasingly the case, perhaps a recording over a loudspeaker is used. When there is a willing piper in the community, he plays a lament, marching slowly back and forth in front of the honour roll. Then he swings his pipes down under his arm and salutes. Usually it is not a snappy, military salute, but more like a friendly farewell.

For more than 30 years now, since I was a young-ster in the Boy's Brigade, I have played the bagpipe on Remembrance Day. I have seen the numbers dwindle and the ceremonies, like the old soldiers themselves, fade away. Standing solemnly before village cenotaphs, I have had a lot of time to ponder the occasion.

One recurring thought has been that in the Canadian climate, the date is a terrible mistake. Inevitably on November 11 the very elements seem traumatized by the enormities of the world wars. Rain, sleet, drizzle, snow, bitterly cold winds—in a kilt, fingers becoming numb, I have endured them all, and sometimes all in the same day. In the past few years, as the aging participants in town ceremonies have been reduced to a handful, and young passers-by cast sideward glances as if witnessing a curiosity, I have wondered if it makes sense to continue to observe Remembrance Day.

Perhaps it is better to forget. It is only a matter of time, in any case, until the names on those rows of white crosses in foreign cemeteries are as forgotten and remote as the names of the warriors who died in the Peloponnesian War. As more and more countries develop the capacity to produce nuclear weapons and ever more lethal devices come off the drawing boards, is there any realistic hope that our remembering or forgetting can to the slightest degree influence the course of world affairs?

The old words, the familiar phrases which used to seem so appropriate, do not really lend themselves to close analysis. We know that reasonably normal young soldiers did not "give up their lives." They were either taken by surprise as a bomb or shell exploded, or else they were dragged from mortal life resisting and struggling to the last breath.

We surely understand now that there are no "glorious" victories, and bemedalled veterans limping along with canes or in wheelchairs cannot be regarded as "winners." War was accurately summed up by the doctor in the powerful film *Bridge on the River Kwai*, who in the final scene climbs up on a hill and shouts "Madness! Madness!"

Voltaire underscored the hypocrisy which war thrusts upon those who presumably uphold the principles of the Judaic-Christian religious tradition with his modification of the Sixth Commandment: Thou shalt not kill, except with the sound of trumpets and in large numbers.

Still, despite all this, I will go on playing the lament on Remembrance Day. The music contains my reason. It is not a celebration, a commemoration or a memorial, but a centuries-old, wordless, plaintive cry to the heavens.

When I look at the people gathered near me, the ones who bear the scars, I know from the expression on their faces that my music speaks for them, gives release to something deeply felt. It expresses protest, protest against the storms of madness which periodically devastate the human race and force the old to perform the unnatural act of burying the young.

For the good of her soul, the woman standing there silently holding a wreath, with her fading memories and increasing loneliness, must register that protest. And in one way or another, so must we all.

Backward Glances at the Old East End

And the Wind at Your Back

Doubting Thomases are in and Good Samaritans are definitely out these days, as people seem to be becoming increasingly cynical, suspicious and motivated by the single driving force of self-interest. Strikes and confrontations are the accepted procedure. Bombing, hostage-taking and hijacking are as prevalent as the common cold. Grab what you can. Every man for himself. And above all, don't take the risk of getting involved in the misfortunes of others. The experiences of Texas truck driver Dick Cockrell not too long ago provide a lurid example.

When the burly ex-marine saw three men openly assaulting a young woman in a roadside park, while other witnesses turned their heads and hurried away, he waded right in, breaking one man's jaw, another's arm, and suffering a knife wound before he disabled the third assailant.

Since then, however, Cockrell has been repeatedly threatened and harassed. "White trash" was painted on the side of his vandalized new car. He has lost 40 pounds, has had to move three times and has had six teeth knocked out in fights. Cockrell, you see, is a white man, and the young woman he rescued is black. Apparently he did not pause to consider that the Ku Klux Klan and other white supremist groups, self-appointed guardians of "traditional American values" and currently seeking recruits among like-minded Canadians, would fearlessly defend the inalienable right to brutalize black women.

Still, says Cockrell of his foolhardy intervention, "I'd do it again in a minute."

My grandmother, who backed down from nothing and who by herself brought eight children across the Atlantic from Scotland on a tramp steamer in 1907, at the time pregnant with my mother, would have heartily approved. "Cast your bread upon the waters," she used to say, meaning that in this life sooner or later you will get back in one way or another what you put in.

I know of one marvellous example, a man called Anthony Dunham. Tall, handsome, good-humoured, he was a pilot in the Royal Air Force during the Battle of Britain at the beginning of the Second World War.

To bolster the morale of the young aviators, families with suitable homes near the air bases used to hold parties whenever there was a lull in the fighting. In one of these families there was a woman who was timid and withdrawn because of a crippled foot. Without really thinking about it, Dunham used to make sure that she was not left out of the merry-making, even persuading her to forget her handicap and get up to dance with him.

When the war ended, the surviving pilots scattered to various parts of the world. Anthony Dunham spent years working in Europe, Australia, the U.S.A., the Canadian North and the province of Quebec, where eventually he found himself jobless and not certain what to do.

Then, of all things, some four decades after the Battle of Britain, he received a telephone call from a British lawyer who explained that he had been tracking him down half-way around the globe for several months. The reason—Dunham had never been forgotten by the English lady with the crippled foot, and she had left him a legacy in her will.

"Aye, quite right," my old grandmother would have responded with a twinkle in her grey-green eyes, "the Lord looks after his ain folk." But I'm not sure that Texas truck driver Dick Cockrell would be totally convinced, not yet anyway. And I'm not sure that it always works out that way myself.

One thing I do know, nevertheless, is that no matter what compensations may or may not come their way in the course of a lifetime, infinitely more precious is the legacy the Dunhams and Cockrells bestow upon their fellow men—the reassurance that human beings are still capable of simple decency.

Keep on truckin', Mr. Cockrell. Old-fashioned perhaps, a little out of date in this age of super highways and eighteen-wheelers, but for you my grandmother would have reserved a special Highland blessing: "May your road be easy and the wind at your back."

Corn Roasts and Communication

The signal which more often than not opens the floodgates of my memories is an odour—the thick, musty scent of ice melting in a street gutter, coal dust by a railway track, lilacs in their short-lived glory, grease used to make French fries, the smell of boiling corn on the cob.

At a corn roast just the other day, as I watched the cooked ears being stacked on plates and fresh ears being plopped into the bubbling water, the rich, creamy fumes transported me back to early childhood and the outdoor Maisonneuve Market on Ontario Street in the East End of Montreal.

There was a huge cauldron on a gas heater and an aproned man dipping a pair of metal pincers into the pot, shaking the water from the corn, sweeping it briskly with a brush soaked in melted butter, then placing it hotdog fashion in a square of waxed paper. We kids could smell that corn from three or four blocks away, and each of us lucky enough to have a nickel . . . But even if a kid didn't have five cents, the man had often been known to accept four or three cents, sometimes even two or one. And every now and again, when he came up with a small ear of corn, he would quickly slip it to a wide-eyed, open-mouthed child who obviously had no pennies at all.

I remember the Gagnon family who lived in a four-room flat along the street from me. We all used to laugh to see the brother and sister about our age sharing a single ear of corn, starting to chew together at opposite ends of the cob. There were 16 children in the Gagnon family, and the father, a construction labourer, did not often have a job during those Great

35

Depression years. The Gagnons knew how to share.

In fact, we all knew a lot about sharing in that period of soup lines and Salvation Army handouts. When my guardian Aunt Janet took sick one time, Madame Bleau, the landlady, came to the door with an enormous bowl of pea soup, which I dined on daily for two weeks. Then I never touched pea soup again for 20 years.

Most of the people in the East End, of course, were French-speaking and originally from rural areas, attracted to the city by the industrial boom during and after the First World War. But there were also pockets of Scots, Irish, Italians, and the children of these immigrant groups grew up with both languages of Canada, and perhaps one or two others as well.

My Aunt Janet was a large, statuesque, broad-shouldered Scottish woman, who used to glide among the stalls of the old market like a ship in full sail, myself a tiny rowboat tugging along behind. She could not have known more than fifty words of French, and the farmers who sold their produce at the market knew even less English, but somehow long conversations used to take place, generously punctuated by gestures and facial expressions.

They wanted to communicate, they had to communicate, and communicate they did.

My aunt got to know all sorts of family details— whose son had broken his arm, whose daughter was going to be married and whose father was at home with a "grippe." When there was a dispute of some sort, an argument over price or quality perhaps, often the people used to come to her to settle it. When my

Aunt Janet died, people from the market and the street filled the Presbyterian Church, scandalizing the minister and elders of the kirk by going down on their knees when a prayer was announced.

It all makes me wonder what is happening now in Quebec and Canada. Many people are fluently bilingual these days, some in high positions in government. But somehow there seems to be a great deal less real communication than there used to be. People of good will are not considered newsworthy and thus are being ignored. Microphones across the land are monopolized by hate-mongers.

Perhaps we need to get together at a corn roast, with not enough corn to go around so that two people will have to share a single ear, the gathering presided over not by a political opportunist but by a man in an apron with a soft spot for hungry kids.

Shortcake in August

Early childhood was not the most serene period of my life, what with my parents' marriage falling apart, constant fights and bickering, and me being shuffled from one place to another. Every year, however, there were the glorious first two weeks of August.

Uncle Jack, who took me in when my parents finally separated, worked for the Canadian Cotton Spool Company in the East End of Montreal, although he and the other employees brought over from Scotland always called it "Coatsies," from J. P. Coats, the name of the parent company in Glasgow. The company's summer vacation period was the first two weeks in August, and apparently some other companies where various of my uncles worked also had holidays during the same two weeks. Uncle Edwin owned an old farmhouse near St. Jean de Matha in the Laurentians. He also owned a car with a rumble seat, and on Friday night when vacation began, my sister, cousins and I, all of us in a state of near hysteria, piled into that seat to go to "the country."

There were no paved roads north of Joliette in those days, but the reduced speed allowed the tantalizing scent of pine trees to whet our appetites. When the car came to a halt in the yard, we kids were off like unguided missiles, racing over the open fields, checking the rock pile with the garter snakes, hopping from stone to stone in the creek, climbing up to the "cut-off" to gaze in wonderment at the vast expanse of forest.

It was pure ecstasy, an electrifying contrast to the cement and asphalt, row houses and three-storey-high wooden sheds, smoke and fumes of the city's East

End. And we knew that mind-boggling delights would come before the two weeks were over. One of these delights was the homemade ice cream of Uncle Al, who had another old farmhouse in the area. Even more wondrous was the annual blackberry shortcake, a ritual in which we all participated.

The high priestess was Aunt Janet, who, following her secret recipe and using an antique wood stove, baked the sponge cake, and all of us kids rushed off to gather the ripe berries. Aunt Gracie walked over to the farm of Monsieur Gravel and bought the required amount of fresh, sweet cream, which could be whipped with a few flips of a fork.

I have eaten baba au rhum and baked Alaska, Black Forest cake and Boston cream pie prepared by the finest of pastry chefs, but nothing since has been quite as magnificent as that blackberry shortcake in the country. To the eyes of small children, it was a white mountain of pure bliss, and we sat around the table staring at it in blubbering anticipation, gulping down our dinners as quickly as we could and agonizing over who would be the first to be served.

Our two weeks in the country always passed too fast, of course, because there was so much to do. Once each week we would all walk to the village of St. Jean de Matha, birthplace of the legendary Quebec strongman, Louis Cyr. While the men lingered at the local hotel and the women did the shopping, we kids explored the town. In those days it was no more than a few frame houses with funny, steep roofs which curled at the bottom. The houses could probably all have been placed inside the huge church. The blacksmith's shop, where massive farm horses were being shod, was the main attraction.

But the surrounding forest was the true wonderland for us. Much of it had never been lumbered. There was no underbrush, and the layers of leaves beneath the giant maples and oaks felt like a plush carpet. It was as if we were walking through a boundless cathedral.

Then came the misery of having to go back to the city, aggravated by the thought that school would soon begin again. I recall that feeling of resentment and despair. I can also recall other traumatic moments of my early childhood, such as walking along Ste. Catherine Street late at night in my pyjamas, holding tightly to the hands of Uncle Jack and Aunt Janet, after a parental donnybrook of some sort. I have heard it said that very young children are unaffected by their parents' marital troubles, but that is simply not true. Even if they do not understand what is happening, they are aware that something is not right, and the anxiety registers.

But much more vivid for me is the memory of climbing into the lap of my large Aunt Janet and the healing comfort of her strong arms around me. Not to mention her awesome blackberry shortcake once a year during the glorious first two weeks of August.

Missing the Summer Exodus

There is one disadvantage to living all the year round, as I do, in a house in the country—I can never have the thrill and excitement of escaping the city and going to a summer cottage for weekends and vacation.

But I know the feeling. I used to live for the weekends, enduring misery through Monday, Tuesday and Wednesday, feeling twinges of anticipation on Thursday, then counting the minutes until the whistle blew on Friday afternoon and I could rush to join the mass exodus of smiling faces on the roads out of Montreal.

The quality of life seemed immeasurably higher in resort spots of the Laurentians and Eastern Townships. People were relaxed and exultant. The air was pine-scented, pure oxygen. The food was mouth-watering. The girls . . . ah, the girls . . . in their sun dresses, shorts and bathing suits they were exquisitely beautiful. And the nights were gentle and long.

Before I was old enough to hitch-hike and fool-hardy enough to buy a motorcycle, apart from the two weeks when I went with relatives to Uncle Ed's place in the Laurentians, I had no choice but to stay in the city and cope with summer the same way as the other people in the East End. The adults used to sit on the balconies along the street, dropping back a cold drink, waiting for a breeze to offset the heat which would continue to radiate from the pavement below long into the night.

Kids had three choices—hang around until a sympathetic fireman took it upon himself to test a fire hydrant, dip into the paper-route money and go to the public baths on Morgan Boulevard, or sneak down to the waterfront and swim in the St. Lawrence River. I never liked the public baths, being forced to shower first and walk through a pan of disinfectant before elbowing and kicking my way into a square foot of water in the crowded pool. I figured that if these precautions had to be taken, there was a fair chance that like other precautions I knew about they wouldn't work, and I would catch something. Something either painful, itchy or embarrassing.

The river, on the other hand, was exciting. It was strictly forbidden to swim in the river. Three or four local children had already drowned. Raw sewage, bunker oil and garbage dumped from the ships in port would float by and had to be avoided if possible. Swimming in the river was blamed for several cases of polio in the area. Those like myself, however, who were lucky enough to avoid that disease, seemed never to get sick at all. The reason, I now realize, is that we probably contacted so many germs in diluted form that we developed resistance to everything. The coddled, scrubbed, disinfected kids who would never have dreamed of swimming in the river were sick all the time. Mumps, measles, chicken pox, scarlet fever, whooping cough—they caught them all.

By my middle teens I had laid out escape routes to the country. Often I found myself among the same gang as back in the city, because groups from various urban districts tended to congregate in the same rural areas. But somehow the country atmosphere, the glorious freedom from office and factory, bus and streetcar, worked a transformation. We laughed, drank, sang and danced till dawn. That is why, I suppose, it took me less than an hour to undertake to buy the house I now live in on Lake Massawippi.

My wife and I had a small apartment in Sherbrooke at the time and another baby on the way. We started out one Saturday morning to look for a larger apartment. When we couldn't find what we wanted, we moved on to the newspaper listings of houses to rent, and I had to ask at a garage how to get to the village of North Hatley.

And there it was, by the lake—space, trees, a big old white clapboard house, countless rooms, wicker chairs on the front veranda, garden tools lying around, the lilacs in full bloom. It was not a rational decision, I admit. I had not intended and really could not afford to buy a house. I didn't even check the plumbing and furnace. But every now and again in a lifetime, the whole of a person's upbringing conspires to make that person act in a certain way.

Still, I made no mistake. The only disadvantage, as I mentioned, is that occasionally during the summer, just for old times' sake, I have to drive up to the big city for a couple of days so that I can join the happy, country-bound exodus on Friday night.

Monsieur Gervais

I sometimes wonder what happened to Monsieur Gervais. He was a pharmacist who lived in the same tenement block as I did when I was a boy in the East End of Montreal, Quartier de Maisonneuve, corner of William David and Adam, two streets up from the waterfront and four streets down from where the tower now droops over the Olympic Stadium like a giant bird with a broken wing.

I am one of those people who remember early childhood. As I have been able to confirm, I can recall details from when I was at most six months old. Monsieur Gervais I remember from four or five years later, when I used to sneak over from my family's section of the back gallery, past the wooden sheds, to where he would sit on a lawn chair after he came home from work. Neither he nor we had lawns, of course, but the back gallery seemed to suffice.

I was a small boy, scruffy, noisy and full of mischief. I once put a rock that I was trying to catapult onto the roof of the flat right through the Gervais's double windows. Nevertheless, he always welcomed me with a warm smile. And he always had something to give me, did Monsieur Gervais—a candy, a sample of a new product, a small toy. I never reflected then on the fact that he and his wife were childless. Nor did it occur to me as we shifted back and forth between English and French that it made any difference what language we spoke.

During those years of the Great Depression people were too concerned about getting enough to eat to worry about language. And they helped one another. When my father, an expert mechanic, bartered tractor repairs for a couple of chickens, he made a huge pot of chicken cacciatore and fed half the people on the block. I can still vividly recall, with diminishing horror, how he slaughtered and cleaned the chickens in the bathtub. And I have told elsewhere how when my aunt took sick a couple of years later, the landlady, old Madame Bleau, came to the door with an equally huge pot of pea soup, which kept my uncle and me going for days.

Not until I started school did I discover that the "French" and "English" were supposed to be different. It wasn't until I read the PQ Government's white paper on the Quebec Policy for Cultural Development that I realized how different. And recently, being forced to witness the willful creation and exploitation of animosity as well as constant bickering over language, I say to myself, ''What happened, Monsieur Gervais? Where did we go wrong?''

My family, like the majority of Scots, Irish, Italians, Greeks and other ethnic groups in the working-class districts of Montreal, lived, played and worked side-by-side with French Canadians. We competed, we fought, we mixed, we intermarried and we survived together. We owned no companies. We never exploited or humiliated one another. Ever since the age of eight when I delivered groceries for *l'épicerie Lagonière*, I have used French as a working language.

You, Paul Gervais, most likely had to use English with your suppliers or at meetings of whatever pharmaceutical organizations to which you may have belonged. Bill 101, the Charter of the French

Language, has justifiably redressed that situation, and
I am in total agreement.

What depresses me, however, is the petty and
adolescent nationalism which is currently being
manifested by some of the "French" in our province
and the stubborn refusal of some of the so-called
"English" to adapt in any way to a changing reality.
I am particularly distressed by the way some politicians distort the truth and exploit fears and
prejudices to promote their own causes. The failure
of the Meech Lake and Charlottetown accords did
not in any way represent the rejection of Quebec's
language and culture by the rest of Canada, as determined separatists would have the people believe.
And the leaders of English Canada who declare that
the majority of Québécois want to break up the
country, so "let Quebec go," are talking nonsense.
Poll after poll has shown that both these positions are
simply false. Is a strain of paranoia spreading across
the land, the first symptoms being a frothing at the
mouth?

We are clearly going through a rough period, in
some respects not unlike the old days of the Great
Depression. Bitterness and small-mindedness on the
part of individuals in positions of influence are
threatening to dry up our fund of good will.

On the other hand, as we have seen before, a little
collaboration, like a few words of a second language,
can go a long way. Quebec must turn its back on the
retrograde tribal nationalism of the independentist
fringe, and English Canada must find the magna-
nimity to guarantee and promote the legitimate rights
of French-speaking citizens. We can't erase the prejudices of certain individuals overnight, to be sure, but

a civilized country must at least prevent people from exercising these prejudices.

It can be done. I know that we're still in the majority, Monsieur Gervais. *Il est grand temps*—it's high time we crossed the back galleries and started pulling together again, *n'est-ce pas?*

Foghorns in the Night

The sound of foghorns in the night, oddly enough, was always a comfort to me. Born and raised right by the Montreal waterfront, I often had my sleep disturbed by the screeching of police sirens or the clanging of railway cars, cranes and machinery on the docks, but the low, robust bellowing of foghorns was always reassuring. It told me that people were taking appropriate measures to avoid disaster and that all was well in the vast, dark outside world.

Many of my boyhood adventures took place in the harbor yards. In the long Canadian winter, when the ice companies used to drive trucks over the frozen river and load blocks to be stored in sawdust for the following summer, I and other neighbourhood children would be sent down with sacks to pick up pieces of coal which had fallen from the railway wagons. We soon learned that if guards or workers were around, a couple of well-aimed snowballs meant having to duck retaliatory hunks of anthracite, but also filling the sack a lot faster. And happy mothers could keep the pot-bellied stoves burning and the kettles boiling in the cold-water flats which lined the district's streets row upon row.

We found ways to sneak by the guards and get to American ships, where sailors with strange accents could be counted upon for gum, oranges, chocolate bars, coloured comic books and perhaps even one of the prized U.S. Navy hats which twisted into a variety of shapes and was worn with matchless swagger.

When I got to be a teenager, I worked on the docks, and a whole new world of adventures and opportunities opened up to me. I talked to seamen from around the globe, ogled pretty girls leaning over the rails of luxury liners, and dreamed of Hong Kong, Shanghai, Singapore and all the other exotic places. I recall one Friday afternoon a sailor on a French ship signalled my friend Roy and me over to an open port-hole when no one else was around, then offered us five bottles of cognac for a dollar apiece. Neither one of us knew anything about expensive cognac—I think we imagined it to be some sort of delicate, light wine for non-serious drinkers—but we did realize that we were getting a deal.

And since Roy's parents were leaving for Plattsburg, New York, for the weekend, we quickly organized a party. To impress the girls I suppose— in those days young men used to do the most ridiculous things just to impress girls—we drank down the cognac in large beer glasses, the kind given away with orders over a certain amount at grocery stores.

The party rose to a peak of boisterousness in remarkably short order. The girls were dancing with wild abandon, and the boys were leering and pawing and knocking around the furniture. Then suddenly the door opened and in walked Roy's parents. They had been unable to find a room in Plattsburg. Repeating to myself a line about the better part of valour from a Shakespeare play we had been studying in school, I took advantage of the consternation to slip through the open door and down the stairs.

I remember that on the sidewalk I was perfectly lucid—I knew the way to go home. The problem was that every time I tried to stand up I fell back down to the cement.

"Look, Mommy, there's a man having an epic fit just like Uncle Jim," a child said to her mother as they hurriedly stepped around me.

"Shut up and keep moving," replied the woman. "The young hoodlums these days . . . It's terrible. I don't know what the world's coming to."

After several futile attempts to stay upright, I realized that I had no choice but to crawl three blocks home on my hands and knees. By noon the next day I was recovering, although I still had trouble focusing my eyes. By late afternoon I had managed to patch the knees in my pants.

I resolved the cognac problem once and for all by deciding never to touch the diabolical stuff again. And during the night I heard the foghorns telling me that despite the menace of my delinquent character, the world was under control.

From Montreal I found my way to the port cities of Glasgow, Scotland, and Detroit, Michigan, and the foghorns came with me, helping me to feel at home in those alien, enormous volcanoes of industrialization. Now, however, I live in the quiet countryside of the Eastern Townships of Quebec, far from harbors and ships.

And oftentimes recently, especially after listening to the late news—massacres in the Middle East, bombs in Ireland, hostage-taking, ethnic cleansing, nuclear reactors falling apart, economic chaos, strikes, acid rain, voluntary and involuntary starvation, mass murder and mayhem—I lie in bed, hoping, naively listening for the sound of a foghorn.

Back to the Old Quebec Heater

Aside from the usual indications that summer is just about over, such as the leaves falling to the ground and the prices of fuel oil and gasoline rising to the sky, in the rural areas of Quebec there is another sure sign that winter is around the corner—the woodpile.

Woodpiles, in fact, are the reaction of country people to the steady and devastating increase in heating costs over the past few years. Thousands have gone back to the pot-bellied stove and wood furnace, and although I once swore that I would never relinquish the safety and convenience of a thermostat, I am being pressured to do the same thing too.

Back-to-nature types and romanticists among my acquaintances tell me that changing from an oil furnace in the basement to a stove in the kitchen has aesthetic and social as well as economic advantages. People sit together and talk to each other again. Souls are warmed along with bodies. A small stack of logs by the back door is a pleasant, rustic sight and permeates the room with the scent of maple, oak and birch.

I remember, however, the old Quebec heater that presided like a black monarch over the kitchen of the East End flat where I was raised. It burned anything—wood, coal, cardboard boxes, corn cobs, old shoes—and together with the black stovepipe which hung from the ceiling and ran along the hallway the whole length of the flat, it was our sole defence against the long, cold winters.

Since my bedroom was at the opposite end of the flat from the kitchen, the frost would build to a half-inch thick on the window pane, and getting out of bed in the morning was torture. But my aunt would have my clothes hanging in front of the stove, and as soon as I had raced down the icy hallway, I must admit that there was exquisite pleasure in pulling on toasted socks, pants and shirt.

During the sub-zero days of mid-winter, it was always a challenge to get enough fuel for the stove. I knew two old couples who burned all their furniture one particularly severe cold spell. And as I've mentioned before, I and other youngsters of the district used to sneak down to the harbor with burlap sacks to scour the railway tracks used by the coal trains. A pleasure of my childhood was to see the joyful look on my Aunt Janet's face when I came home with a sackful of anthracite rescued from the fate of stoking a ship's furnace.

The old pot-bellied stoves were dangerous, of course. Occasionally one would explode or simply fall apart, and half a block of tenements would burn down. The stovepipes were also a menace. It was always touch and go whether they would catch on fire before the annual spring cleaning, which occurred between the arrival of the first boat in Montreal harbour, winner of the Gold Cane, and the flooding of Notre Dame Street.

A girl in the block where I lived once decided to take advantage of her parents' absence over a weekend and throw a big party. All the local teenagers were invited, and somebody came up with the idea of a jitter-bugging contest. Before long feet were stomping, bodies were gyrating, the floors were bouncing, and the walls were vibrating. I recall looking up the instant before it happened. One of the suspension wires holding up the hallway stovepipe had come loose, and two sections of the pipe were sinking at a joint. The first three-foot length landed on the head of a blonde-haired girl in a white blouse, tartan skirt and white bobby socks. She virtually disappeared in a cloud of thick, black soot. All I could make out were the bobby socks.

Then section after section of the overloaded pipe came tumbling down, each one adding new dimensions to the all-engulfing soot storm. Screaming, choking girls and youths were rushing out the front and back doors of the flat.

My Aunt Janet flew into a fury terrible to behold, but soon I was in the bathtub and my clothes were in the wash. I never did find out how the parents of our hostess reacted when they returned from their weekend vacation.

Why I am less than enthusiastic about reverting to a stove should now be clear. The problem, however, is that soon there may be no choice. Under the careful supervision of both provincial and federal governments, oil prices may simply rise to the point where thermostats, like Learjets and Lincoln Continentals, are the playthings of the wealthy.

But when the time comes, I'll make sure that the stovepipes are securely attached to the ceiling, and I will permit no rock 'n' roll on the premises. And I will be careful not to become too attached to the furniture.

The Spirit of Christmas

As the Christmas season arrives, the men and women of the Salvation Army appear on the streets again with their bells and donation pots, and I find it quite impossible to pass by without digging into my pockets.

For reasons which have nothing whatsoever to do with theology, I have always felt close to the Salvation Army. Actually, the flat where I was born and raised happened to be right next door to the Sally Ann meeting hall, and many of my childhood adventures took place in the yard behind it. Despite the fact that my guardian aunt was a staunch, Scottish Presbyterian, she occasionally attended services at the Salvation Army, and I was allowed to take part in various functions. The pastor when World War II broke out was a Major William Marsh, who had four sons, Joe, Woodrow, Finney and Ross, the last of whom was my age and a childhood playmate.

It was Finney, however, who for some reason has been haunting my thoughts in recent weeks. I vividly recall seeing him in his Royal Canadian Air Force uniform before he, along with other Canadian and a few American volunteers, left to fight in the first great clash for control of the skies, the ''Battle of Britain.'' To Ross and me he was a man of mature years, our idol, but I realize now that he could not have been more than 19 or 20 years old at the time.

Even more poignant is the thought that if Finney had survived the war, he would now be more than 75 years old. And I have a feeling that he, along with many another of the idealistic, dynamic youths who volunteered to go to war and did not return, would

have become an excellent community or national
leader.

As Eleanor Roosevelt once astutely observed, the
losses of war in terms of society in general are not felt
until 40 years or so after the event, when so many of
the natural leaders who should have been, are simply
not there.

When the telegram arrived to inform the Marshes
that their son had been shot down over Singapore and
was presumed dead, both Ross and I were too young to
grasp the full meaning. We were confused. Finney had
done a wonderful, heroic thing, we were told, and we
should be proud and happy, yet in the faces of his
parents and other adults we could clearly see that
something was horribly wrong. I think it was then that
I started to dislike the hymn ''Onward Christian
Soldiers,'' without really understanding why. I became
an avid reader of war dispatches in the newspapers,
grieving over the losses and sometimes feeling terror
that I and everyone I knew would soon be killed.

I remember the Marsh family in the tiny Salvation
Army band, which used to play Christmas carols at the
corner of the street as the snowflakes fluttered down
through the light of the street lamp and settled on their
capes and bonnets and on top of the base drum.

My aunt and uncle used to marvel at the audacity
of the little group of Sally Ann musicians. We were in
a tough, mainly French Catholic district during a
period of turmoil. Like the isolationists in the U.S.,
many French Canadians were opposed to involvement in a European conflict, while the English-
speaking people, largely of British stock, felt just as
strongly that their duty was to help the mother

country. French-English tensions were exploited, just as they still are, by various politicians and community leaders, sometimes leading to gang fights and riots.

But no one bothered the handful of Salvation Army people as they stood on the street corner, and I knew the reason. I used to see the derelicts with newspapers stuffed into their shirts to keep warm coming to the door of the meeting hall, and sometimes the pastor (who was from Newfoundland, I believe) would ask me to interpret when he couldn't understand the street French. But French, English or whatever, anyone who knocked on the door of the red brick meeting hall was sure to receive food and clothing, and the people of the East End of Montreal learned to respect the Salvation Army.

That is the reason why a Sally Ann woman, all alone and in her quaint little bonnet, could walk into the smoke-filled male preserve of a beer parlour, packed with sailors and stevedores and foul-mouthed rowdies in every stage of drunkenness, and actually be cheered as she passed around the collection box. The Salvation Army can be proud of its more than a century of good works in North America. Presumably, as the name indicates, the organization's primary objective is to save souls. But to me, especially in these times of renewed tensions and economic hardship, the Sally Ann represents the transcending of barriers which divide man from man as well as genuine, down-to-earth acts of charity.

It also represents individual self-sacrifice, and in the timeless carols played by a small band of musicians standing in the snow on a street corner, spreading good will to all, the true spirit of Christmas.

Explaining Snow

Outside my window the snow is falling so thickly that the huge maple tree a few feet away is now just a dark grey blur on a slightly luminous grey canvas. Already three or four inches have piled up on the window sill.

If he were here today, the boy on the Caribbean island of Antigua who once startled me by asking me to explain snow, would understand immediately. At the time of our talk, I used every description and device which came into my head, smashing an ice cube and spreading the chips on the table top, telling him to imagine that the grains of sand on the beach were white, cold, fluffy and falling from the sky.

"Don't worry about it," I said finally. "Enjoy the sun and the sea. Snow is a misery. Why do you think people come here in the winter? There's no snow in paradise."

Yet when I was a boy, I loved snow. It padded the asphalt and cement, transforming the bleak city streets and lanes into a vast playground. Once the ploughs had passed a few times, forts could be built between the sidewalks and roads, with secret chambers to stockpile snowballs and elaborate systems of connecting tunnels.

As the snow packed down and hardened, all the streets became hockey rinks where games lasted from early morning until the cries of mothers from balconies and front doors announced the last minute of play. In vacant lots, fathers and older boys shovelled the snow into alpine slopes which challenged the daring of youngsters with sleds, toboggans or simply scrap pieces of tin or wood. The true daredevils engaged in the dangerous sport of grabbing the back bumpers of passing cars and hanging on as long as possible.

With the approach of Christmas, glorious Christmas, the coloured lights appeared, in windows, on doors, hanging from trees, looking so incredibly beautiful and promising when they twinkled through the falling snow.

But as I grew older, snow and ice began to lose a lot of their charm. The disillusionment probably started the day when, driving my first car, I was blinded by a cloud of blowing snow, jammed on the brakes and skidded across the road into a telephone pole. There's nothing quite like that feeling of help-lessness and the awful nausea in the pit of the stomach when your car is skidding out of control and the wipers clear the windshield just enough for you to see what you're going to hit.

In time I mastered the tricks of winter driving, to some extent at least, and did not find myself in the ditch more than five or six times a year. But other troubles blew in with the winter snows, such as the ice sliding off the roof of my house and severing the electricity and telephone lines. Or the arthritic pains in the ankle I fractured in a motorcycle accident some 30 years ago.

The ankle was aching the day of a heavy snow-storm a few years ago when a student from central Africa came into my office. Unlike the boy in Antigua, he knew exactly what snow was because he had just trudged through a mile or two of it, but he could not believe that it would ever go away.

"We will all surely die," he moaned. "It keeps coming down. Soon it will cover up the trees and the buildings, and we will all be buried and freeze to death."

"No no," I responded, laughing off his panic. "In three or four months spring will come and all the snow will disappear."

"Are you sure?" he asked.

"Of course I'm sure."

He gazed out the window at the wild swirls of snowflakes now being churned by a rising wind, winced, shivered, then shook his head.

"You Canadians," he said in a sing-song accent, "are a very trusting and long-suffering people. You allow yourselves to be exploited by the British, then the Americans and just about anybody else who takes the notion, you elect and re-elect federal and provincial governments which mismanage your affairs and treat you with disdain, you tolerate extremists and revolutionaries who openly announce that they intend to tear apart your prosperous and wonderful nation, and you even trust your atrocious weather."

"I suppose that's true," was all I could think to say. "You see, we know that no matter how bad everything gets, no matter how much snow falls, sooner or later it will be gone."

"And you'll still be here,'" he added.

"Right," I said, "we'll still be here. And so will the country."

Tourtières and Shortbread

Quebec tourtières, thick, juicy, steaming in a mist of spicy, appetizing aromas, and richly delicious Scottish shortbread—these are the two foods permanently associated in my mind with Christmas.

When I was a small boy back in the early 1940s, one of my aunts, Tante Alice, originally from a village near Trois Rivières, used to hold a traditional family *réveillon*, or Christmas Eve dinner. The Roman Catholic side of the family arrived after Midnight Mass, while the Scottish Presbyterian side wandered over after a "Watchnight" service. I remember the twinkling of the Christmas lights through the snowflakes and how I used to run off every now and again to explore a fort in the huge snowbanks between the streets and sidewalks.

But especially I remember the two foods so tantalizingly good that there could never be any question of eating enough of them: Tante Alice's tourtières and Aunt Janet's shortbread. Purists will explain that the original tourtières were made of tourtes, a wild pigeon which is now extinct, but the tourtières which I devoured so eagerly were pies made of minced fat pork and cooked in an oven. And according to Tante Alice, she made them exactly the way her grandmother used to.

A steady diet of these pork pies and shortbread, made of butter and eggs and all the other things teeming with cholesterol and triglycerides, would, I suppose, be a guarantee of premature cardiac arrest, but nobody knew about that in those days. And another thing we did not know anything about, living in that dark era before the publication of the Parti

Québécois's white paper on Cultural Development, is
that we were engaging in thoughtless and wanton
contamination of cultures.

Quebec tourtières and Scottish shortbread, not to
mention Italian ravioli, Polish gwonki, Irish stew and
English steak-and-kidney pie—it's no wonder that I
grew up with such a lack of commitment to nationalist causes and cultural exclusiveness. I have even
been known, it may as well be confessed, occasionally to slip into Chinese restaurants or delicatessens
selling smoked, spiced kosher corned beef,
commonly known as smoked meat or *la viande
fumée*, and I would probably sell my soul for a
heaping dish of Trinidadian curried chicken and rice.

I was once asked to describe "soul food" to a
Black man, who had been raised on a French-
speaking island in the Caribbean and therefore knew
nothing of the American South. Another time I found
myself explaining the difference between Hebrew
and Yiddish to a Jew. And most recently, with a group
of young Québécois intellectuals, it turned out, of all
things, that I was the only one who actually knew the
taste of genuine tourtieres.

With so many good things to share, then, why is
there a never-ending fuss about culture in Quebec?
Why do spokesmen from both francophone and
anglophone communities keep ranting about threats
to their cultural survival? Frankly, I think the explanation is that these spokesmen, in their messianic
enthusiasm, have distorted the true nature and
function of social culture.

Each individual's identity, of course, is determined by the culture or cultures by which he or she is

conditioned. Cultural identity, therefore, allows individuals and groups to know who they are and that they are different from one another, which is fine. The essential function of any culture, however, is not to isolate people from each other but rather to permit individuals to survive by adapting to the realities around them, including people who are different. Since the realities are constantly changing, cultures cannot remain static. They must also change constantly. A viable culture is neither a barrier to human relations nor a hothouse flower which will shrivel and die if the door is left open. It is a set of tested practices and values which allow a person to live a meaningful life among other human beings.

It is a passport, providing the individual with the identification needed to be enriched by moving among the various other cultures of the world. Whatever progress the human race has made over the ages has been the result of the mixing of cultures, of cross-cultural fertilization, which often enough has taken place in defiance of the dictates of various ayatollahs, ministers of state and self-styled custodians of sterile cultural purity, which is non-existent in any case.

One need only think of the Renaissance, triggered by the blending of Eastern and European ideas, of American jazz, of turkey dinners, or of Marco Polo bringing back from China the pasta recipe which would become the mainstay of the marvellous Italian cuisine, once the tomato was brought to Europe from the New World.

Quebec, indeed the whole of Canada, has been uniquely blessed by the blending of cultures, and the holiday season is the time to take advantage of this

blessing. Myself, I'll be having shortbread and tourtières, and whatever else happens to catch my eye.

White Christmas

Patriotism for the "True North" and Bing Crosby's mellow tones notwithstanding, I am less than enthusiastic about a white Christmas. With only a few days to go this year, already there is more than a foot of snow on the ground. and the heavy grey sky is unloading again. The radio has just announced that all schools in the area have been closed, meaning that the peace and tranquillity of thousands of mothers will be cruelly shattered for the day.

Yesterday I froze my fingers and toes trying to get my car to start, but that was a minor inconvenience compared to what happened to my neighbour. Another car skidded into his at an icy intersection, mangling the left fender and door to the tune of $540 in damages. In Quebec French there is a perfect expression for it—*"c'est pas un cadeau."* Literally meaning "It's not a gift," this expression corresponds more or less to "It's no bed of roses" or "It's no picnic." And even though gifts are expressly associated with Christmas, when one considers the implications of a white one—treacherous roads, soaring fuel bills, roofs and walks to shovel, electricity blackouts—*vraiment c'est pas un cadeau.*

The first time I experienced a non-white Christmas was when I went to the University of Glasgow as an exchange student. The smog was so thick that I had to shinny up the posts to read the street signs, but there wasn't a trace of snow, and I have the most delightful memories of that Scottish yuletide.

Another student I had chanced to meet a few days earlier invited me, a poor Canadian boy alone and far from home, to her place for dinner. Originally from a place called Carrickfergus in Ireland and with the intriguing name of Sheelagh, she was an attractive, vivacious girl with long, strawberry-blonde hair. Those were the days when young ladies still wore dresses and nylon stockings, and I vividly recall how dazzling she looked as she stood at the top of the stairs, dispelling the smog with a radiant smile of season's greetings.

My modest gift to her was a calendar illustrated with the usual, spectacular Canadian landscapes, which someone had conveniently sent over to me. Her gift, of all things, was a box of chocolates. Delicious chocolates they were, and she popped one into my mouth from time to time as we snuggled on the sofa, doing our bit to promote international relations. On that first non-white Christmas, I didn't miss the snow one bit.

Since then I've had occasion to spend the holidays in the Caribbean a few times, sitting under a palm tree in shorts, sipping a rum punch, watching the pelicans dive-bomb the fish from out of a cloudless sky. My wife would make a little Christmas tree with various tropical pine branches, and the kids would have a great time decorating it after they got back from water-skiing or wind-surfing. No one seemed in the least concerned about being deprived of a white Christmas. The whole mystique is misguided in any case. Surely there was no snow on the roof of the stable when Jesus was born. And it wouldn't surprise me if Bing Crosby made his famous recording inside an air-conditioned studio in sunny California, afterwards donning a cap and sunglasses to have a round of golf.

But as I've mentioned elsewhere, we did have white Christmases when I was a boy in the East End of Montreal. I remember the wonderful snowbanks between the streets and the sidewalks. Sometimes they were four or five feet high, perfect sites for mazes of tunnels and forts. The neighbours used to get together in those days and shovel the snow into what seemed an enormous mountain on a vacant lot. A few buckets of water would transform the snow pile into a slope for tobogganing and sledding, and we kids used to spend hours and hours climbing up and sliding down in absolute ecstasies.

Christmas Day, for me, was usually spent entirely on Adam Street between Sicard and LaSalle. The aunt and uncle who brought me up would first visit another of my eight aunts. Gifts were exchanged, and we youngsters were allowed to indulge ourselves in shortbread, fruit cake, biscuits, ginger ale and all manner of tasty delights.

Then we would stroll back along the street, exchanging best wishes with acquaintances along the way, to my grandmother's flat, where numerous other relatives were gathering to celebrate. Then came more gifts, and eventually a big Christmas dinner with pie for dessert.

Finally, clutching our treasures in our arms, we would walk home, exhausted from all the excitement but satisfied and happy. More often than not it would be snowing, and I remember how the street lamps, decorations and strings of coloured lights in the windows and doors glittered merrily as the snowflakes floated down. To a small boy, it was powerful magic, the transformation of the dull, grimy city street into a wonderland.

Come to think of it, perhaps after all there is something to be said for a white Christmas.

Spring Patience

Like grey hair and far-sightedness, patience is not something commonly acquired at birth. It slowly invades over the years, infiltrating the fortress of your personality when you're not looking, then one day, when your old-age pension cheque is a few days late perhaps, you suddenly realize that you have it.

As a youngster I could never wait for spring to take its natural course. In the East End in those days, the snow was piled in banks between the streets and sidewalks during the winter, and the streets and side-walks themselves became layered with a granite-like mixture of packed ice and grit.

The first definite sign of spring was always an icebreaker ploughing a channel in the St. Lawrence River, signalling the start of the race for the Gold Cane, which is awarded to the first ship of the year to dock in Montreal Harbor. Nowadays, with reinforced hulls, electronic gear and all the rest, it is more like a hundred-yard dash. The winner is likely to slide into a berth one tenth of a second after midnight New Year's Eve. Fifty years ago, the Gold Cane race was an exciting, meaningful event. We would all watch gleefully the first ship plying its way up the river, the pilot manoeuvring the vessel to bypass ice floes, often being forced to wait until an ice dam broke up. But we all knew that the sight of that ship meant the miracle of spring.

That was when I and the rest of the kids in the district got out our axes and shovels. Neither we nor our parents seemed to realize that taxes were being paid to the city to hire workers for street maintenance. We did the job ourselves. After all, they were our streets. We would compete with one another, chopping the hard-packed ice and shovelling it into the middle of the street to be crushed by passing vehicles. Then, our impatience reaching a peak, we would actually sweep the sidewalks, and before long they were clean and dry and gleaming in the spring sunshine.

I was also impatient for church services to end. I would count everything that could be counted—the congregation, the lights, the stained-glass window panes, the organ pipes. During especially long-winded sermons I used to experience a recurring and terrifying fantasy. I would stare at the chandeliers hanging by chains from the huge wooden beams which arched across the ceiling of the church, and I imagined myself climbing on a window sill, leaping up and grabbing one of the chandeliers, then swinging from one to another across the sacred building.

I knew at the time that such an outrageous act would surely mean eternal damnation. And even worse, it would mortify my large Aunt Janet sitting in the pew beside me. But the urge was overwhelming, almost irresistible. My muscles would twitch, and as the minister droned on, I would grit my teeth and wrestle with the demon within me. By the time the service was over, I would be an emotional wreck, which probably explains why the minister had the curious delusion that I was a deeply religious kid.

But the years have taught me the virtue of patience. Now I can sit serenely through university convocations, political addresses, academic conferences and various other events with the maximum interest level of a dripping faucet. When a recorded message in English and French informs me that all the Air Canada people are busy and that I should hold the line until an agent becomes available, I simply hum along with the schmaltzy music or else read a book or two until my turn comes up.

Not too long ago, while taking a shortcut around New York City, I got into a monumental traffic jam. It seemed as if the entire automotive production of Detroit, Japan, Italy, Germany and Sweden was lined up bumper-to-bumper in three lanes behind and in front of me. But I used the occasion to clean the windows, add a quart of oil, adjust the idling, tighten the hose clamps, clean out the glove compartment and all the other little chores I had been meaning to do but had never gotten around to.

I have definitely become a patient man as I've grown older. The explanation, I imagine, is that when you're young you want to speed things up, but when you get older you want to slow them down. Still, this morning I went out to check the drains around the house and found them blocked with ice. Without thinking, I grabbed a pick axe and started chopping furiously. After all, it's supposed to be spring. The sun is supposed to be doing its job.

I guess I haven't fully acquired the virtue of patience yet. Or perhaps when Canadians are finally convinced that spring is just around the corner, having had to wait so many months, we simply can't restrain ourselves from nudging it a little.

End of an Era in the East End

The last time I drove to the East End of Montreal, twice I found myself going the wrong way on what are now one-way streets. Then I couldn't stop at half the places I wanted to visit because no parking spaces were available. When I was a youngster growing up in the area during the late 1930s and early 1940s, there were no one-way streets and no parking problems. The reason, of course, was that few people owned cars. In fact, I doubt if it ever occurred to any of us kids that an ordinary resident could even think about owning an automobile. Neither did we imagine that hot water could come out of taps or that flats could be heated other than by pot-bellied stoves or huge, cast-iron kitchen ranges.

Normally it took four strong men to lift one of those ranges, although I remember the time when our next-door neighbour, Mr. McGuire, picked his up in a fit of rage after he had lost his job, carried it down the hallway to the front room and hurled it through a third-storey window. It barely missed a passing milk wagon, and for days afterwards people came from all parts of the districts of Maisonneuve and Hochelaga to marvel at the gaping pit in the asphalt of Leclaire Street between Ontario and Lafontaine.

We depended, I suppose, on that sort of event for entertainment in those pre-television, pre–rock-concert days. The simple pleasures, you might say. We had several good riots, especially after the war started and the zoot-suiters descended like a swarm of locusts. They were anti-conscriptionists, if not exactly pacifists, and they wore outlandish jackets with large lapels, shoulders padded a yard wide, tightly pegged pants, pointed shoes and long watch chains which swung down to their knees. The mere sight of a zoot-suiter sent East-Enders of British stock into something akin to the feeding frenzy of sharks.

More memorable perhaps were the epic battles between local boys known to everyone, such as the formal boxing match at the East End Boys' Club featuring Big Dick Gamble and Jack Keenan. Jack's opponent was supposed to have been a boxer from Point St. Charles or Verdun, but he didn't show up, so Dick Gamble had to fill in at the last minute. Toe to toe they stood and slugged it out round after round, the bout ending in a draw. The Keenan brothers were all handy with their fists, and they were at their most ferocious when they were fighting each other, a fairly regular occurrence. But the rough-and-tough character of the district made it an excellent training ground for future athletes. Among those who graduated to the CFL, for instance, were Moe Bremner, Gordie Rowlands, Larry Fairholm and my own nephew Bruce Wilkins.

The end of the era probably came with the bitter strike at Canadian Vickers Ltd., one of the largest employers in the East End and the company which had been responsible for attracting so many English-speaking workers from Glasgow and Belfast and various other industrial centres of Great Britain in the first place. The strike was an extravaganza of entertainment, even by local standards. First there were the redecoration hit squads who visited the homes of managers and executives with buckets of paint. In a kind of preview of modern spray techniques, with a single whoosh the paint was applied to ceilings, walls, carpets and furniture without recourse to brush.

Then came the saga of the scabs, busloads of whom the company attempted to bring into the idled plant. The strikers, naturally, tried to block these buses, and the climax came one afternoon when a mere handful of men, using logs as levers, actually overturned a fully loaded bus. Mind you, they were not ordinary men. One of them was my brother-in-law Keith Wilkins, who weighed in at around 230 pounds, and he looked like an underfed schoolboy beside Lloyd Welcher, who was six-foot-six, around 300 pounds, and could pop off the cap of a beer bottle with a flip of his cucumber-sized thumb. Then there was Lloyd's friend "Tiny"—he wasn't from the East End and I never knew his real name, but suffice it to say that *he* made *Lloyd* look small.

The Vickers' strike ended an era, I believe, because it marked the disappearance of working-class complacency and resignation. No longer were people willing to accept that cold-water flats, fish and chips, long work hours, periodic lay-offs without pay, and streetcars were their God-ordained lot in life. The people developed greater expectations.

These greater expectations spurred the exodus of the English-speaking population of the East End of Montreal—to the South Shore, out west and else-where. But as I saw the other day, just as in similar districts the world over, I imagine, life goes on. Current residents of the East End, having learned to cope with one-way streets and parking problems, no doubt have even greater expectations than the population they replaced. I wonder where they will go.

The Montreal of My Youth

City of Symbols

The City of Montreal, if not exactly in the best shape financially, is at least rich in symbols. An old French-Canadian story tells of a farmer, visiting the metropolis for the first time, who was taken to see the Notre-Dame Church at Place d'Armes. Asked what he thought of the church, the farmer replied that it was *"assez belle"*—quite nice. Then his gaze wandered across the square to the substantial stone pillars of the Bank of Montreal, and he added, "Mais c'est un maudzit beau presbytère"—But that's a damned beautiful manse.

In the eyes of many French-speaking Canadians, the two buildings, a church and a bank, accurately symbolized French Canada and English Canada. People built monuments to the gods which they worshipped.

Montreal writers have long used the mountain and the river symbolically. Solid and permanently established, the rich lived on the mountain heights while the poor occupied the flats by the river, constantly moving and menaced by floods. Then there was always "the other side of the tracks," such as the District of St-Henri, described by Gabrielle Roy in her celebrated novel *The Tin Flute*, where the residents did not even have a view of the illuminated cross on the mountain to inspire them. The cross faced the East End of the city, and the people there probably needed it more, because they were sandwiched between two parallel railway tracks, one below Notre-Dame Street and the other above Ontario Street.

At one time, when the Sunlife Building was still the tallest structure in the British Commonwealth, its mass of square grey stone dominated one side of the mountain, while St. Joseph's Oratory rose in white, rounded purity on the green slopes of the other side. The first, with its falcons sweeping down on the pigeons below, perfectly represented the ruthless world of finance, while the Shrine, with its steps strewn with abandoned crutches and braces, and the heart of Brother André preserved in a glass container, was a symbol of the miraculous power of religious faith.

When I was a youngster in the East End of Montreal, two features of the area became particularly engraved in my mind. One was the Jacques Cartier Bridge, and the other was the open space just below Sherbrooke Street between Pie IX Boulevard and the railway tracks east of Viau. This vacant area served as a vast, makeshift playground, a jungle for safaris, a wasteland to be explored, where hostile Indians, desperadoes in black hats and sabre-toothed tigers lurked in every thicket. There was also the mystery of the ruins—great slabs of granite, almost hidden by the weeds and bushes, which had clearly been set in place by intelligent beings.

In the imagination of child adventurers, the slabs were remnants of an ancient civilization, hauled there by Druids or Egyptians or people from the far reaches of Westmount or N.D.G., perhaps even Ontario. We were told by our elders, however, that they were simply the beginnings of a great stadium which had been planned for the British Empire Games, then cancelled when the Second World War broke out. Some 40 years later the great stadium finally did get built on exactly that spot, and it soon became another symbol. The "Big Owe" is a monument to mismanagement and corruption, to what used to be called "*pots de vin*"—graft and kickbacks. In fact, the Olympic Stadium, Place Ville Marie and various other skyscrapers now overshadow many of the old symbols, and whereas the latter seemed to underline the divisions between French and English, more recent buildings are either sterile or have negative connotations.

But the Jacques Cartier Bridge, despite the mutilation it suffered so that the St. Lawrence Seaway could pass under its tail, remains a positive and dominant emblem of Montreal. In the old days we kids used to walk across it to the rural haven of St. Helen's Island, with pockets full of pebbles which we would vainly try to drop down the funnels of ships passing below. To us the bridge meant escape from an enclosed world and the chance to meet new people.

Bridges have a special beauty and symbolism. They represent union, the transcending of barriers, the crossing over from one place to another and from one community to another. The last time I crossed the Jacques Cartier Bridge it took a full hour, and I heard on the radio that the other bridges were just as congested. That is one of the facts about living on an island, notably the Island of Montreal in the Province of Quebec. From both the practical and symbolic standpoints, it is essential to have enough bridges.

Poison-Ivy Summer

"Summer"—in Canada it is still a magic word, conjuring up images of multicoloured blossoms against a background of lush green, the rising sun turning the blue of a country lake into shimmering gold, long gentle days to warm the marrow of winter-weary bones. For me, however, these images are always tempered by the thought of toxicodendron radicans, "a climbing shrub having glossy, variously notched trifoliate leaves, greenish flowers, whitish berries," otherwise known as poison ivy.

My experience with this diabolical wonder of nature began when I was working on a pipeline in the East End of Montreal. Healthy, character-building labour it was, slinging a pick and shovel all day in the fresh air and sunshine, getting the good earth under my fingernails, tanning, sweating, nurturing a mighty thirst, then gathering with the boys to participate in the restorative miracle of a cold beer after the whistle blew.

My other activity that summer was playing in the pipe band of the 401 Fighter Squadron RCAF, which meant practices at night during the week and parades and competitions on weekends. In fact, the Friday morning that my boss sent me and another worker out to scythe the tall grass in the path of the pipeline, I was in an exultant mood, because that evening the band was leaving for the Highland Games in Fergus, Ontario. Tomorrow our drummers would beat a crisp double roll, the perfectly tuned pipes would strike up as sweetly as the sea birds singing, and the band would glide majestically across the competition field, amid the roar of the crowd, on its way to another championship. At night, surrounded by bevies of leggy Highland dancers and pretty young things drawn to the spectacle of kilted masculinity, we would celebrate.

Little did it matter that full Highland dress—thick woollen kilts and hose, heavy jackets, balmorals, shoulder plaids, leather belts—was not the ideal garb for a hot summer day. The crowd loved it, and as my grandmother used to say, honest sweat never hurt an honest man.

All morning while we cut grass I regaled my partner with stories. He was swinging the scythe like a madman in his envy. At the noon whistle we both sprawled in a shady spot to eat our lunches, neither of us paying much attention to the little climbing shrub with trifoliate leaves and whitish berries.

When my arms and hands began to itch on Saturday morning, I speculated that the CNR was probably using some cheap soap to wash the sheets of the sleeping-car berths. It was the hottest day Fergus had ever had for its Highland Games. Not a whisper of a breeze. The half-naked spectators sat in the shade fanning themselves, while we bandsmen, in full uniform, silver buckles and badges flashing, sweat pouring from our brows so that sometimes we could barely see, marched back and forth under the blazing sun.

By the time I got back to the hotel, I was in agony. Every part of my body—my eyelids, under my arms, in-between my fingers and toes—was covered with red spots and blisters. It was the classic, the ultimate, shaping up to be quite probably the first terminal case of poison ivy. The band officer, normally capable of sending a man with multiple leg fractures on a route march, called for a military ambulance.

I eventually found myself in the Queen Mary Veterans Hospital, being treated with oatmeal baths and lying under a tent of damp gauze, which dried up the blisters when the water evaporated. Profound embarrassment now replaced the infernal itching. In the ward were men still suffering from the wounds of three wars, one with an arm and leg missing, another paralyzed, another finally having a piece of shrapnel removed from his back. Groups of ladies from various service organizations wandered through the ward every day, bringing cheer and gifts. They would gather around my bed, peer at the gauze tent and mutter sympathetically: "He looks so young . . . How dreadful . . . Very likely that new chemical warfare they're using . . . Maybe he was gassed . . . Radiation for sure . . . Don't get too close, Mabel."

I lay still with my eyes tightly shut, pretending that I was in a coma. Cigarettes—remember the old flat fifties?—candy bars, decks of cards, New Testaments and magazines piled up on my night table. I even got the autographs of Maurice Rocket Richard and Elmer Lach, again not daring to open my mouth in case I had to explain what had happened to me.

Then it dawned on me that somehow I was making more money than ever before. My pipeline salary and full RCAF pay continued simultaneously, plus compensations and benefits, and it was costing nothing for room and board. In fact, once the itching lessened and I was able to look at the nurses properly, I was not eager to get back to the ditch and my hairy colleagues of the pick and shovel, and to halve my earning power at the same time.

When the lights were low at night I slipped into the medicine dispensary, splattered myself with iodine and claimed a total relapse, but that did not fool the doctor, I'm afraid. I was discharged and escorted to the door.

This story, of course, is not intended to discourage anyone from enjoying the wonderful summer, the revitalizing warmth, the moonlit lakes, the odour of the pine trees, the intense joy of a vacation in the great outdoors.

But keep in mind that if you take a notion to romp in the meadows or stroll along a country lane, you should watch out for three-leaf shrubs, especially if there's a chance that you may be working up a sweat.

The Disappearing Pipe Band

When Claude Charron was obliged to resign from the Quebec National Assembly after a conviction for theft and various other acts unbecoming a lawmaker, the people of Quebec had special pause to reflect on how our governments, while grossly mismanaging public funds, can efficiently and generously look after their own. At the age of 35, Charron retired on an indexed pension of some $27,000 a year, to begin immediately. Since he could presumably resume his law career, or begin another career, like so many others who have withdrawn or been removed from public service, he could simply invest his pension so that by the time he reaches the ordinary worker's retirement age of 65, he should easily have a tidy little nest egg of two million dollars or so. Hundreds of other former politicians, of course, are in the same position, although few beginning to dip into the pot quite so young as Charron.

Meanwhile, government budget deficits and accumulated debts are in the stratosphere, unemployment and salary cuts are rampant, and economists are warning that unless something is done soon, both federal and provincial pension funds for the common citizen will dry up in a few years. It all makes me think of the time when the 401 Fighter Squadron RCAF pipe band disappeared.

I was a member of the band, and we were leading a parade along Sherbrooke Street. When we reached the reviewing stand, loaded with air vice-marshals, generals, admirals and various other brass-plated dignitaries, we halted. Then the bandsmen each did a left turn, and the band moved ten paces to the side of the street opposite the stand. Next we about-turned to face the stand, continuing to play while all the units marched by.

The band consisted of 12 pipers four abreast in three rows, a bass drummer between two tenors, then a last row of four side drummers. Turned sideways, only three pipers and two drummers were in the front row. Our Pipe Major, wanting to make the best impression on the brass in the reviewing stand, decided to beef up the row facing the stand. He signalled for two pipers and a drummer to shift positions so that five pipers and three drummers would be in the temporary front line.

That was fine until the parade had passed, when the bandsmen were supposed to move forward into the middle of the street again, then turn left and march off. At the command, we started to move forward. Then one of the pipers who had been moved to pad the front line facing the stand decided to slip back to his regular position. But another piper had already stepped into that position. A side drummer, also trying to get back into his usual spot, bumped into the bass drum. In the next few seconds, there was total confusion. Bandsmen were literally wandering in all directions, as the generals, admirals and air vice-marshals looked down in astonishment.

I can recall thinking that I had to escape somehow, and evidently the other members of the band had exactly the same thought at the same time. Each of us pushed his way into the crowd, and the pipe band simply disappeared.

Our Drum Major, a wonderful guy but a stickler for discipline, was appalled. Fortunately, however, he couldn't say much because he was himself in a state of disgrace, having a few weeks earlier nearly wiped out single-handedly the senior officers of the Canadian Armed Forces at the Tri-Service Ball. The band had travelled to the Festival of Britain the previous summer, and he had been intrigued by the way the British Drum Majors tossed their maces into the air and caught them as they strutted in front of their bands. Twice in Montreal when he tried to imitate the feat, crowds lining the sides of Ste. Catherine Street, he missed the catch, and the band had to mark time red-faced as he bent his bulky, kilted frame to pick up the mace from the pavement.

Those drops must have loosened the heavy metal crown of the mace, because when our Drum Major took a notion to twirl it over his head at the Tri-Service Ball, the top flew off and headed straight for the table of honoured guests. By some miracle, all of the officers ducked in time, and I imagine that they are now collecting their pensions.

Whether there will be anything left in the pot for those of us who are still working, however, is now highly uncertain. The keepers of the pot, our government representatives, have set themselves up nicely, to be sure. Some of them are even likely to become millionaires.

And the rest of us poor slobs? Well, we can try to trust our leaders, try to do what we're told to do. But it's beginning to look as if we may eventually find ourselves, like my old pipe band in front of the reviewing stand on Sherbrooke Street, in a state of total confusion, the only course of action being to duck into the crowd and disappear.

A Music Master

To my ears, most of the music which transports my children and grandchildren into trances is not nearly as melodious as a railway train clanking down a crooked track. I have also occasionally been less than overwhelmed by high-brow recitals which connoisseurs claimed were master performances. But if there is one musical phenomenon which brings joy to young and old, expert and ignorant, rich and poor in almost every country of the world, it is a good marching band. Drum Majors strutting with their maces, majorettes prancing, the bass drum booming out the beat, the rows of bandsmen gliding by with their heads held high—everyone loves a parade.

How many parade spectators, however, think about the tremendous amount of hard work which goes into producing a high-calibre band, particularly on the part of the music directors, who are seldom dealing with musical prodigies? I believe that special medals should be given to the musicians who direct bands, for extraordinary patience and dedication, for fighting juvenile delinquency by offering young people something meaningful and exciting to do, and for increasing the collective happiness of the human race.

Recently I had a reunion with such a musician, a man who is in fact one of the living legends of Montreal. The majority of Montrealers no doubt have never heard of Alec McNeill, but in his special artistic field, the classical music of the Highland bagpipe known as "piobaireachd," he is revered by piping enthusiasts throughout the world.

84

It runs in the family. Alec's father, Archie McNeill, was the famous "Blind Piper of Glasgow," whose compositions are certainly among the most popular ever written for the instrument. Cousin Seumas McNeill, of the College of Piping as well as of the Physics Department of the University of Glasgow, is a leading authority on pipe music in Great Britain and is active in broadcasting and recording.

In the early 1950s, Alec McNeill became Pipe Major of the 401 (City of Westmount) Auxiliary Squadron RCAF pipe band, of which I was a member. We were a motley crew of music makers when he took over—beginners and veterans, immigrant Scots, Canadians, Irish, one Englishman and one French Canadian—and I suppose that we were still a motley crew a couple of years later, but by then we were winning all the championships in eastern North America.

When we met again, my two old friends and fellow pipers Wendell MacLean and Angus MacDowell, Alec and myself, we reminisced about the tunes of glory, and we played a few of them as well. Each of us remembered the miracle experienced many times at Highland Games in years gone by. After practising and competing all day long in full uniform, marching countless miles, not being able to eat or rest, feet numb and every muscle aching, we would be in a state of near collapse as the massed bands lined up on the field for the announcement of the band contest results.

Then the loudspeaker would blare out the words: "Winner of the Grade One March, Strathspey and Reel Competition—The Four Hundred and First

Royal Canadian . . ." And that's when the miracle took place. A dancer would step in front of the band to carry the championship cup, the drums would rumble a double roll, and suddenly, like a rocket lifting from a launching pad, the total exhaustion, the aches and pains, would fly away. Each of us felt a foot taller as the band paraded off the competition field. It was more like floating than marching, and fingers which were limp only moments before danced over the pipe chanters . . . and we all knew that those exquisite moments of triumph and profound satisfaction would not be happening without the genius of Alec McNeill.

Individually we were much like the musicians in the other good bands—the 48th Highlanders and the old Caber Feidh from Toronto, the Toronto Scottish, the Worcester Highlanders from Massachusetts—but Alec had arranged the music and trained us to play as one man. Equally important, his sensitive ear and skills as a reed maker allowed him to set the instruments in harmony.

How they hated us in Toronto in those days. A rag-bag conglomeration of musicians from French Montreal was not supposed to win all the prizes. But when Alec McNeill stepped up on the boards to play in the individual Open Piobaireachd Competition, every serious piper gathered around to listen in awe. Ironically, the man regarded as the master player, the Glenn Gould of piping in North America, could never make a living with his musical gifts. The only full-time employment for a piper is in a military band. Alec held regular jobs in the CNR and then at Zellers, and he did all of his teaching, practising and band training at night and on weekends.

When I think back now, I realize how much my life was enriched by being in a band. In my teens I travelled throughout eastern Canada and the United States. and I even found myself in Scotland and England during the Festival of Britain. I met fascinating people from every walk of life. Our own band was composed of high-school dropouts and university professors, artists, salesmen, office workers, mechanics, tradesmen and students. But at the command "Quick March," we were all on precisely the same wave length.

Whatever the uniform, whatever the instrument, marching bands represent not only a universal level of entertainment, but also a system of positive values—discipline, teamwork, responsibility and the striving for artistic perfection. Few band musicians ever become virtuoso performers, but because of the efforts of gifted masters like Pipe Major Alec McNeill, who willingly sacrifice their time to train and to lead bands, they become better human beings.

And everyone can continue to enjoy parades.

The RCAF Squadrons of Montreal

For the veteran fighter pilots of the two squadrons of greater Montreal, the sight of a Hawker Hurricane Mark IV with the old RCAF insignia swooping down to within 150 feet of Sherbrooke Street turned the clock back more than four decades. The two local squadrons—No. 401 "City of Westmount" and No. 438 "City of Montreal"—both formed in September 1934, were celebrating their 50th anniversary with a three-day reunion. The white-haired men gazing up at the vintage war plane had participated in the legendary Battle of Britain and the ensuing air combats which wiped out the German Luftwaffe in World War II. They had served with distinction, amassing countless honours and decorations, and they had created many legends of their own.

Personally, my greatest thrill of the reunion came at the banquet held in Hangar 10 of the St. Hubert Armed Forces Base. After more than a quarter century, I and other surviving members of the old 401 Squadron RCAF pipe band marched again. The resounding cheer which reverberated through that vast hangar provided one of those rare moments in a lifetime when the concerns of the everyday world vanish and a person hovers in a mist of euphoria. As our band circled the floor, surprising ourselves by how well we could still play, I glanced back to see the veterans of 401 falling in behind, led by Wing Commander Wendell Reid, the Squadron CO who had brought the pipe band into the RCAF some 35 years earlier.

Most of the bandsmen were callow teenagers at the time when we were enlisted as a group shortly after the war. A few adjustments were made to birth-dates and other details, because the squadron was determined to acquire a ready-made pipe band. No one seemed particularly concerned about these details, since it was clear that we were not expected to have anything to do with flying planes. We regarded the officers as senior citizens, as well as slightly mad. In reality, of course, the majority of them were in their twenties and thirties, and I realize now that quite a few were struggling to readjust to ordinary life after having spent the early years of adulthood undergoing an experience of incredible intensity and danger. They were the young men who scrambled on those tiny British air fields, rising into the sky to intercept a formidable 20th-century flying armada, knowing each time they took off that some would not be coming back.

Relations between the band and the squadron did not always run smoothly at first. The Drum Major, Captain Bob Bulger, and the Band Officer, Flight Lieutenant Joe Dooner, surely must have despaired of ever teaching pipers and drummers a modicum of military discipline. One problem was that, unlike the Army, the Air Force had no established procedures for the integration of a pipe band. The blue RCAF tartan of our kilts was a recent innovation, and when the bandsmen were not actually on parade, about all the officers in command could come up with for us to do was guard duty and clean-up detail, both of which we resented with a passion.

We were primarily interested in winning band competitions, and in fact the 401 Squadron pipe band eventually did win every major trophy in eastern North America. But occasionally we used to think that we were doing so in spite of the RCAF, which was more concerned about the way we marched, saluted, shined our shoes, polished our buttons, and cut our hair than the way we played our musical instruments.

After all these years, however, I know now that the squadron was in fact immensely proud of the band. That became absolutely clear when we stepped onto the hangar floor at the reunion in St. Hubert. Pipe Major Alec McNeill, the man who guided the band to its apex, was there, as well as pipers Wendell MacLean, Angus MacDowell and Bev Campbell, all still living in the Montreal area. Drummers Reid Scrimgeour, Phil Brady and Jackie Barber returned from the U.S. for the occasion. Wilt Sheehan drove down from the Laurentians, while his brother Larry, Andy Hurd and Gaston Brazeau came back from Ontario.

Naturally we all spent a lot of time reminiscing about the old days—the trips, the triumphs, the disasters, the sprees, the girls we left behind. It was difficult to believe that 33 years had passed since the band represented Canada in the Festival of Britain, participating in the famous "March of the 1000 Pipers" along Princes Street in Edinburgh. We took about 16 hours to fly over in an unpressurized and unheated RCAF DC 4 called the North Star, stopping to refuel at Labrador and Iceland.

Before we left Montreal an airman just back from Britain tipped us off that we should take along as many pairs of nylon stockings as we could afford. British girls were desperate for nylons, he said, and sure enough, they were. Ah, those were the days all right . . . We feared that the Scots might laugh at us, upstarts from Quebec wearing an artificial tartan and playing a non-traditional tune like the *RCAF March Past*. But they didn't laugh, they cheered wildly. Every time we paraded, people crowded around us shouting "Canada! Canada! Hooray for the Canadian Air Force!" Men handed us drinks and women rushed out and embraced us as we tried to maintain ranks marching along the street.

The Royal Canadian Air Force, we soon found out, was held in high esteem. And we all realized, of course, that we had the slightly mad senior citizens of our squadron and all the other RCAF squadrons to thank for that. We were reaping the rewards of their heroism.

But along with the old Spitfire and Hurricane aircraft, the 401 "City of Westmount" Fighter Squadron has now become a museum piece. On June 22nd, 1996, the squadron paraded its colours for the last time before being disbanded, bringing to a close an illustrious segment of Canadian aviation history, a segment marked by a weird and wonderful alliance between pipers and pilots.

High School Closing

A man in his mid-forties with an aura of congeniality about him, he was standing at the doorway of a hall in Calgary, where I had just delivered a talk on contemporary Quebec.

"You don't recognize me, do you?" he asked, smiling.

I shook my head.

"The last time I heard you was in 1950," he continued, "when you gave the valedictory address . . . I'm Zen Kolisnyk."

Then it all came back to me. Zen Kolisnyk, a Ukrainian Canadian, and I, of Scottish and Italian parents—we had been the somewhat oddball winners of the Jewish Women's League Prize at the graduation ceremonies of the High School of Montreal in 1950. Brought up in the St. Urbain Street district and now an engineer in Western Canada, Zen had not heard that our old high school had been closed.

As we reminisced, it occurred to me that I had lost track of many of my former classmates other than John DeNora, Alec Stirling, Bill Doran and Jimmy Angrave, who were all in the teaching profession as I was. Dave Duchesneau, my close friend in those high school days, had joined the U.S. armed forces and had been killed in a helicopter crash shortly afterwards. I knew that Dimitri Tjelios, whose desk had been just behind my own, was with Bell Telephone, that my old chess partner, Eugene Husaruk, played violin with the Montreal Symphony Orchestra, that Dennis Palko had his own engineering firm handling contracts from around the world, and that Dick Lee owned Chinese restaurants in Montreal.

During our high school years, the girls, of course, were kept separated from the boys in the other half of the building on University Street, teenaged goddesses to be worshipped from a distance, generating wondrous fantasies in those days when something was still left to the imagination. I did manage to get to know a few of them—Margaret Twyman, Joyce Penny, Connie Anderson, Anita Rasmussen—brief, awkward encounters, but not forgotten.

As I think back, I realize that the system, the discipline, the teachers of Montreal High during the late 1940s were truly excellent. I and a handful of other students from the District of Maisonneuve used to travel at least an hour on the streetcar to get there, but it was worth our while. I also realize now that the High School of Montreal was more than a school. It was a spirit, a statement about the nation of Canada, an experience of living with an extraordinary conglomeration of the various races and ethnic groups which make up this country. In the graduating class of 1950 alone, there were people of British, French, Chinese, Italian, Greek, Syrian, Ukrainian, Polish, German, Hungarian, Japanese, African and Jewish extraction, to mention only the more evident.

Off in Calgary, Alberta, engineer Zen Kolisnyk was concerned about what was happening in Quebec and Canada, about divisions and animosities resulting from Quebec nationalism. I tried to reassure him. But in the back of my mind certain phrases from PQ Government's White Paper on Quebec's Cultural Development Policy jarred my train of thought, much as the clanging of railway cars in the dockyards used to disturb my sleep as a child.

"*Un étourdissant chassé-croisé*"—a dizzying hodgepodge—"*une sorte de caravansérail*"—a kind of eastern hotel frequented by foreigners—these are two of the phrases used to describe what is considered to be the deplorable state of the City of Montreal by spokesmen of the PQ. Extreme nationalists in Quebec apparently have a dream of some kind of ethnic purity, and they seem increasingly determined to pursue that dream, which as citizens of the free country of Canada they have the right to do.

At the same time, however, Zen Kolisnyk and I have a right to say that we too have a dream, a dream nurtured in the classrooms and corridors of the old High School of Montreal and which, incredible as it may seem to the more ardent tribal nationalists of Quebec, actually incorporates the few positive elements of their own vision. Our dream is of a nation extending from the Atlantic to the Pacific, where different peoples, including French-speaking Canadians as a distinct group, can be themselves, live and let live in mutual respect, dignity and harmony, enriching one another by their diversity, creating a new concept of pluralistic nationhood.

The High School of Montreal is closed now, but the spirit of tolerance and brotherhood it engendered in me and you, Zen Kolisnyk, and in many other kids from the tenement districts of Montreal, is the glue that will hold this country together. Make no mistake about it.

Montreal Revisited Through Germany

A letter from a German translator reminded me that there was a time not so long ago when dialogue between English-speaking and French-speaking Montrealers was often characterized by nasty expressions. The German is translating my novel *Snow Lark*, or *Suzanne* as it came to be called after the feature film was made, most of which takes place in the East End of Montreal during the Second World War and the resulting Conscription Crisis. With a French-Canadian Catholic mother and a Scottish Presbyterian father, Suzanne is caught in the no-man's land dividing the French and *Les Anglais* when tensions between the two groups often erupt in fist-fights and brawls. Concerned about the conditions and distorted values which led to this physical violence, while writing the book I never gave much thought to the linguistic violence. I simply recorded what I used to hear.

Then the letter arrived from Germany asking me to explain various expressions used by the characters in the book. The first question was: "Does *pepsi* refer to the French, or does it mean sissy, softy, etc.?" The German translator was curious to know if the word had any connection with a popular cola drink. Having never hung around restaurants in a French-speaking working-class area of Montreal, he had of course never heard the standard afternoon-break request; *"Un Mae West pis un pepsi."*

He was equally curious about *maudzit bloke*, and I had to explain that like Southern Americans with the expression "damn Yankee," many east-end Montrealers

95

grew up without knowing that the term consisted of two words. "How about 'joe bastard'?" wrote the translator. "'Joe' sounds English, and yet the context makes clear that the term refers to the French. What is the etymology of the phrase?" Sticklers for precision, those Germans. But I had no idea of the etymology. He went on to observe that he could not find the word *marde*, used in a number of expressions in my novel, in any of his dictionaries. Here I simply referred him to Pierre Trudeau, and I added that I was once asked to converse in English with a Quebec bishop so that he could get into practise for an upcoming ecumenical congress. The bishop had learned his English as a hotel bellhop, and he spoke quite fluently, except for one thing—he kept using the English for *merde*, or *marde* as it is pronounced in Quebec, as the mild, inoffensive expletive it is in French. It's no wonder that those ecumenical get-togethers never got off the ground.

Explaining "The Dirty Main" brought back childhood memories of hanging onto the hand of my substantial Aunt Janet as she forged a path through the sailors, longshoremen and painted ladies of lower St. Lawrence Boulevard on our way to the old Montreal General Hospital for stitches or repairs of one sort or another. I still have the desk which she bought for $5 in a used-furniture store on the "Dirty Main." She had great ambitions for me, God bless her.

In the novel there are descriptions of how the inside staircases leading from the second-floor balconies to the third floor of tenement flats provided cosy, secluded places for teenagers wanting to "fool around." Apparently Germans use ground floor for first floor, first floor for our second floor, and so the translator had trouble visualizing exactly where the inside and outside staircases were located. He also had no idea what "sugarbags" were, and probably many contemporary Montrealers would not know about the corps of "Zouaves," symbolic papal body-guards who used to march in the Corpus Christi parades. They wore baggy grey pants with a red stripe and were hardly the favourites of Protestant hard-liners, especially those whose sons were overseas on military duty.

The easiest expression to explain was N.D.G., although as a child I doubt if I knew what the initials stood for myself. For East Enders in those days Notre-Dame de Grâce was a remote outpost on the other side of the city where everybody spoke English. You could get there by means of a long journey on the 3A Ste. Catherine streetcar, but you might never get back again.

Neither will Montrealers, fortunately, ever go back again to the absence of communication between the "English" and the "French" communities of the 1940s and 50s. These days one hears lamentations about the general deterioration of relations between the two main language groups of Quebec, but after being obliged to explain to a German translator the bitter verbal and social realities of Montreal 50 or so years ago, I know for a fact that we have actually made progress.

In particular, Anglo-Quebeckers have become largely bilingual, therefore much more aware of the francophone realities. Religion no longer creates the barriers it used to create. Communities, institutions, businesses and cultural activities are becoming increasingly mixed. Various political and community leaders, to be sure, are still trying to exacerbate animosities and create divisions between the ethnic groups of Montreal and the rest of Quebec. But the future will be decided by the people in the street, and in Montreal, most of the people in the street seem to be moving in the right direction.

My Great Scoop

In every walk of life there are the triumphs, however small or momentary they may be, which keep a person going. A waitress gets a generous tip, a businessman swings a big deal, a truck driver meets a pretty waitress, and she gets another big tip, a politician gets a compliment. For a newspaperman, triumph is a scoop.

During the hot summer of 1956, when I was a cub reporter for the late *Montreal Star*, I managed to pull off a genuine scoop, and to this day the thought of it helps to keep me going.

I began journalism the old, traditional way—not through college courses but at a desk all day monitoring the police radio. Then I graduated to the morgue beat, which if nothing else kept my appetite within the bounds of the purchasing power of my meagre salary. Eventually, after hammering out with two fingers hundreds of one- and two-paragraph minor items, I was given a real assignment—covering a pharmaceutical conference at the Mount Royal Hotel. The thrill of that first by-line overshadowed even the conference's public relations officer, a Swedish beauty with long blonde hair hanging over one eye Veronica-Lake style, who practically took me into her arms as I walked through the hotel door.

My big scoop, however, came many weeks later, and I must admit that Olga, another pretty and talented blonde and the daughter of the Russian lady who owned the rooming house where I lived, had a lot to do with it. I knew a little Russian, and she inspired me to learn a little more.

When McGill and l'Université de Montréal jointly hosted the International Congress of Entomology that summer, as a by-then experienced reporter of dull conferences, I was assigned to it. The first thing I did was check in a dictionary to learn that an entomologist is an expert on insects, or a "bug man," as the other reporters put it.

Then I discovered that entomologists from the Soviet Union were at the congress. Since the Cold War was raging at the time, contacts with people from behind the Iron Curtain were quite rare and eagerly sought after by reporters. I also discovered that the Soviet scientists were of two distinct types—small or medium-sized scholarly-looking men in thick glasses, or huge men with bulges all over who didn't say much but showed great concern for the welfare and privacy of their more delicate colleagues. The Russian delegation was staying at the old Laurentian Hotel, and when they held a press conference, I astounded everybody by popping a carefully rehearsed question in Russian, something about wheat production, I think. One of the scholarly scientists responded excitedly, bypassing the interpreter and launching into a long speech directly to me. I pretended to take copious notes. The big men took careful note of me. But, of course, not having understood a fraction of what was said, I had no story.

The next day at the congress, however, I bumped into the Russian who had replied to my pretend question, and he took me aside, this time speaking slowly. To my astonishment, he said that he had something interesting and important to tell me and suggested that I come to his hotel room, after 11 p.m., using the back staircase in the hotel. His heavier-set colleagues, he remarked, were generally in conference at the hotel bar at that time.

Naturally I took Olga. It was right out of a James Bond movie. We had a coffee at the hotel restaurant, exited arm-in-arm with eyes only for each other, strolled slowly along the corridor as if heading for the elevators and our room. Then, when we were sure the coast was clear, we darted up the stairs and over to the room where five Russian entomologists were waiting with bottles of vodka.

I had to wait for the scoop. Olga was one of those leggy ladies who seem never to be fully contained by a skirt, and for the first 20 minutes the conversation focused on her nylons. Apparently Russian girls did not have nylon stockings in those days, and it was the considered scientific conclusion of the five assembled "bug men" that such stockings looked good on a shapely pair of legs. But before the session ended, I did get three notebooks full of information, on current research, on threats to various crops, on production problems, and on how the Soviet Union, according to all five of the entomologists, despite the famous "five-year plans," would be dependent on imports of Canadian wheat for as long as they could see into the future.

Finally, the man who had invited me up to the room, a Dr. Steinberg, spoke up. He proudly announced that he was the grandson of Nicholas Rimsky-Korsakov. In the next few minutes he told me many intriguing anecdotes about the world-renowned composer, and in the late edition the following afternoon, I had my first front-page newspaper story.

It's all relative, of course. But for many days during that long-ago summer of morgues, scientists, deadlines and beautiful blondes, I felt as if I had personally written "The Flight of the Bumblebee." And it is still one of my favourite compositions.

Birthday Party at The Ritz

The woman on the telephone told me that her name was Phyllis O'Reilly and asked me if I knew her husband, Gerry. I replied that the only Gerry O'Reilly I had ever known was a guy back in the Maisonneuve district of the East End of Montreal some 30 years ago.

"That's the one," she said. "We're having a surprise birthday party for him—cocktails and dinner next Friday in the ballroom of the Ritz Carlton Hotel."

Ballroom of the Ritz! The last time I had heard of Gerry O'Reilly he was driving a taxi, and along with a few other East Enders he was occasionally involved in the dubious business of distributing pinball machines. I might have expected a reunion at Harry's smoked-meat joint, the Starland Tavern, or maybe the Café de l'Est.

"Does your husband have a sister named Mildred?" I asked the woman on the phone, still thinking that there had to be some mistake.

"Yes. Mildred will be at the party. Roy Love is coming up from Corning, New York, Chico Sofonio from Palm Springs, California, and Gloria Anderson—she's married to Dr. Chen Tsai, who used to work with Wilder Penfield—they're flying in from Portland, Oregon."

Bells began to ring as faces from long ago flashed into my mind. It was the same Gerry O'Reilly all right, no doubt about that. As I hung up the phone I remembered that he used to have an unusual escape gimmick. The way for girls to get out of the East End was to marry well.

103

For boys it was usually hockey, football or boxing. Gerry O'Reilly, however, used to travel to the United States and try out for baseball teams. He was a good player, but so far as I knew he had never beat out the vast competition for the big leagues.

The ballroom of the Ritz was already packed when I arrived. For a few moments I began again to think there had been some mistake, because I couldn't recognize anyone. Then suddenly the thrill of rediscovery wiped out more than a quarter century of adult life. Roy Love was there, and so were Mildred, Chico, Gloria and Gerry himself. For a few hours that night we were kids again, prowling the streets between Pie IX Boulevard and Viau, necking in the back seats of the Granada and Odeon movie houses, jitter-bugging at the East End Boys Club or the Maples, reliving wild parties and the various other escapades of our youth. Roy Love was on the back of my Ariel 500-twin motorcycle again, hanging on for dear life as we swung around streetcars. Chico and I were picking up girls and heading for Ideal Beach in his old Chevvy.

The whole evening was a triumphant success. One of Gerry O'Reilly's sons, a true chip off the old block, was master of ceremonies, and speakers reminisced in English and French about the various stages of Gerry's life and career. His baseball buddies were there, as well as classmates from the old Catholic High School of Montreal, the one where students went who couldn't make it into Loyola.

And, of course, there were his many business associates, because Gerry O'Reilly was president of Alouette Amusements Canada Inc., a company which handles the now-booming enterprise of video games.

When I first found that out, I glanced over at Roy and Chico, and from the looks on their faces I could tell that all three of us at the same time had a vision of battered pinball machines being loaded onto the back of a pickup truck. Who would have thought?

For that matter, who would have thought that anybody from the tiny English-speaking minority of Montreal's working-class East End would get anywhere in life? Brought up during the wartime years of violent confrontation between English and French, in an area where neither Protestant nor Catholic Anglophones had a high school, gang fighting seemed to be what we could do best.

On the other hand, maybe we learned something. We knew who we were—the children of factory workers from the industrial centres of Scotland, Ireland, England, Italy and other European countries— and we learned how to survive in an overwhelmingly French Quebec. A lot of us are still here.

English-speaking Quebeckers in general have been accused by Quebec independentists of being unwilling to adapt to reality, the "new" French reality of contemporary Quebec. It is true that a few business leaders and wealthy people from the West End have abandoned the province.

It is a pity, however, that the independentists could not have attended the birthday party for Gerry O'Reilly at the Ritz. They would have realized that anglophone Quebeckers from the working-class areas of the province, the majority of the minority, adapted to the French reality long ago, that they have always been ready and willing to work with their fran-cophone co-citizens, and that working together is far more productive than childish confrontation.

The Full Catastrophe—Wife,
House and Kids

American-Canadian Thanksgiving

Like that of millions of hapless turkeys, my fate, or at least that considerable part of it which has to do with a wife, five children and family life, was settled by a Thanksgiving dinner.

I was a graduate student at Wayne State University in idyllic downtown Detroit at the time, trying to survive on the few dollars I earned as a teaching assistant, supplemented by fees for occasional weekend gigs as a musician and regular dips into the shrinking bank account I had miraculously squeezed from my summer job as a newspaper reporter.

Wayne State University, sight unseen, had been my choice simply because it offered the largest fellowship, but I soon learned two things not mentioned in the students' handbook: big U.S. cities are not cheap places to live, and the campus itself had been conceived as an "urban renewal" project, otherwise known as slum clearance.

The project, however, was only partially completed, and out-of-town students had to find lodgings in what remained of the slums. As the demolition proceeded, rats, cockroaches, pensioners, derelicts, addicts and scholars were coralled into a steadily increasing concentration, right in the middle of a city where gunshots were as common as car horns and mugging was the customary form of social interaction, but that is another story.

An active and normal 23-year-old in those days, my main concern was getting enough to eat, so that I would have the strength to pursue my other concerns. A few weeks into the autumn semester, I realized that

I was beginning to weaken. Then one day as I walked down a street, cautiously as usual, fingering the change in my pocket to determine whether I had enough for both a hamburger and a piece of pie, I heard joyous polka music coming from a meeting hall. Now in downtown Detroit back in the 1950s, one normally minded one's own business, the city having already won the urban-homicide championship and needing no more numbers. But the music from the hall, then successive waves of tantalizing odours rolling over me like surf on a Caribbean beach, exerted an irresistible attraction. I stepped back one pace, only to catch a whiff of some exotic dish and take two steps forward. Eventually I was inside the door, and I discovered that I had stumbled upon a Polish-American wedding reception. Then somebody grabbed my hand, shook it heartily, and ushered me into the crowd. Another invited me to sit down at a table loaded with steaming, gastronomical delights. And that was only the first course.

I found out that day how it is remarkably simple to slip into a wedding feast. The groom's people all presume that you are a guest of the bride's family, and vice versa. The technique is to smile and shake hands all around, kiss the ladies, wave to people across the room from time to time, as if they were old friends, and eat with gusto.

The only hitch, of course, is that weddings generally take place on weekends. By imitating the desert camel, I could take on enough food to sustain me until Wednesday. Thursdays were bleak. Until, that is, Thanksgiving Day came along.

I knew about Thanksgiving Day in the United States. In fact, I and another student, Tom Duffy, a marathon runner who was constantly ravenous, had planned to pool our resources and have a go at roasting a chicken. But at the last moment his coach invited him to dinner, and he left me at the starting line without so much as a backward glance.

The bitterly cold, damp winds were already sweeping in from the Great Lakes and down the long, broad corridors of the Motor City's main thoroughfares. I turned up my collar and felt thoroughly miserable as I trudged to class the day before Thanksgiving. Not a chance of a wedding either, I moaned to myself, Americans traditionally celebrating the occasion at home with family.

After teaching my class, I was about to leave when I noticed that one of the co-eds had lingered behind. Actually she happened to be the most attractive girl in the class, a shapely, long-legged, raven-haired and soft-eyed beauty from the hills of Kentucky. Many thousands of people from the poorer areas of Appalachia had migrated to Detroit.

"Miss," I said, managing to smile despite my gloomy mood and deteriorating condition, "is there something I can do for you?"

"Yes, sir," she replied, shyly averting her large eyes.

"Continue," I said. I was struggling to maintain a proper professorial tone and appropriate academic distance.

"Well, you see, sir, I was aiming to . . . you know . . . where I come from . . . most anywhere in the States I reckon . . . when there's a stranger alone . . ." Then she blurted it out: "Would you like to have Thanksgiving dinner with my folks?"

Turkey done to a turn, heaps of stuffing, roast potatoes, tender corn, candied yams, black-eyed peas, mashed turnip, cole slaw, slices of sugar-cured ham, buttered carrots, ending up with pecan pie and freshly whipped cream—I was totally overwhelmed.

There was, naturally, nothing else to do. After a decent interval and one more Thanksgiving dinner, I asked that thoughtful girl to marry me. At our wedding reception in a small hall, the radiant beauty of my bride transformed darkest, dingiest downtown Detroit into a wonderland of brightness and joy. To this day, that is the image of the infamous motor city which sticks in my mind.

And let me add that there is one marvellous advantage to marriages between Americans and Canadians. Thanksgiving Day in Canada is the second Monday in October, while in the USA it falls on the fourth Thursday in November. With a lot to be thankful for, I have always felt it my solemn duty to celebrate both.

Christmas of the Big Snows

If you have enough of them, there's no better point of reference than the birth of one of your children to keep dates of various happenings clear in your mind. I distinctly remember, for example, 1966-67 as the winter of the big snows, because in December 1966 my fifth child and only son was born. As I write today, a few snowflakes are falling outside my window, and for more reasons than one I think fondly of three decades ago.

So far this year I haven't really needed my thoroughly winterized, four-wheel-drive vehicle, but I certainly could have used it back in 1966. At that time I owned a battered old Volkswagen. Nowadays more often than not I drive alone, but I recall when my wife and I and the five kids would be crammed into the tiny car, a mishmash of arms and legs and chewing gum and dirty diapers, and it seemed that most of the other cars on the road were huge station wagons, each with a solitary driver.

On a cold day with the heater going full blast, the inside of the old Volks would begin to warm up at just about the end of a ten-mile journey. Generally it got me to where I wanted to go, but not always. Driving over a country road in rural Quebec through a blizzard one day, I finally had to pull over to the four-foot snowbank when the wipers could no longer move the snow piling on the windshield. I waited for a few minutes, expecting that such a violent storm would soon let up, but it simply intensified. So I decided to abandon the car and walk to a nearby farmhouse, where I could phone home and wait in relative comfort.

That was a mistake. Although I still maintain that my reasoning was reasonable—to remain in the automobile with the motor running meant the risk of carbon monoxide poisoning, while to shut off the motor meant the possibility of freezing to death. In addition, I knew how the snowplough operators drove when the snow was heavy and the visibility near zero—they simply got up a good speed and leaned the plough slightly into the bank. I had terrifying visions of what would happen if a snowplough came along while I was sitting in my nearly buried little blue car.

I pulled the hood of my parka over my head and walked away from the car, battling the wind and snow with each step as if I were moving under water. After about 20 paces, it dawned on me that I could not see where I was going. The snow was now so heavy and the wind so strong that I actually could not make out the hand at the end of my arm. I decided to get back to the car.

I'm still not sure whether it was panic or sheer bloody-mindedness which overcame me when I couldn't find the car. I can recall conjuring up images of my frozen body being found on the road, then laughing out loud and thinking, what a stupid way to go.

By this time I was trudging aimlessly through the drifts with outstretched arms, and to my profound relief I eventually struck metal. I groped for the door handle and jumped into the car, congratulating myself now for extraordinary control and endurance. As my eyes thawed, however, I realized that with parka and beard covered in snow and looking something like the abominable snowman, I was not in the right car.

Someone else had been forced to stop a little ahead of me on the road.

The driver did not notice me at first. He was gripping the steering wheel and staring at the darkened windshield, seemingly mesmerized, repeating to himself *"Chrisse de tempête"* and a few other expressions typical in French Canada.

"Tabarnacle!" he screamed when I tapped him on the shoulder, then he tried to hurl himself through the other side of his car.

At a school board meeting a few days later, when my wife's time was fast approaching, my anxiety about getting her over 20 miles of snow-bound country roads to the maternity ward must have been transparent.

"Don't worry about it," Doug Martin, one of my fellow board members finally said, "just call me any time day or night."

"What do you mean?" I asked.

"I drive a snowplough," he explained.

Well, from then on I didn't worry. It might even be intriguing, I speculated, for my baby to be born in a snowplough. But as it turned out, despite two feet of new snow on Christmas Day, the weather settled down, and when labour pains began on December 26, 1966, I was able to drive my wife to the hospital all by myself.

And although, like all parents I suppose, there are occasions when I have my doubts, that's how I got the best, if a bit belated, Christmas present a man could ever hope for, in the winter of the big snows.

Becoming a Millionaire

Each day that I walk around the little Appalachian town in Quebec where I have lived for more than 30 years, I am reminded of how easily I could have become a millionaire. My Kentucky-born wife, Jean, used to do the reminding, telling me that if I had listened to her and not been such a damned fool, I could have been collecting dividends instead of counting discount coupons and raiding the penny jar to mail a letter.

This week, for instance, one of my neighbours announced that he was putting his cottage up for sale. I was dumbfounded to find out that the asking price is $247,000. When I moved to town, the place was selling for $5,000. Another neighbour has a price tag of $275,000 on a house which I could have bought in the mid-sixties for about $12,000. The man who delivers the eggs once tried to sell me his farm for $10,000, all equipment included. Now he wants $100,000 for the land alone. Of course, I didn't have $10,000 at the time, but as my wife pointed out, I could have borrowed it from the bank at an interest rate that by today's standards was an act of charity.

I admire people who can make money with their wits. My brother-in-law in Michigan adds $10,000 or more a year to his salary just buying and selling. Not too long ago he noticed that a large department store was having a clearance sale of eight-track cassette players which attach to a sound system. The price had been reduced by half to about $75, and he decided it was time to investigate.

115

When he got to the store and looked around, he saw that all the cassette players had already been sold. But his hillbilly horse-trader instinct told Roy to hang around a bit, and sure enough, in came a man with one of the machines under his arm. My wife's brother sidled over.

"Pardon me," he said to the man, "is that one of those eight-track cassette players they had on sale?"

"Yeah," the man replied. "I goofed. Thought it worked all by itself, but you gotta hook it up to a hi-fi, which I ain't got. I hope they'll take it back."

"One way to make sure of that," said Roy helpfully. "Just tell 'em you tried it out and it don't work."

That's exactly what the man did, and he smiled at my brother-in-law gratefully as he walked off with his refund. Roy then waited for a few minutes, checking the prices on various other items in the store, and eventually he went over to the counter and asked to buy one of the eight-track cassette players on sale.

"Sorry, sir, they're all sold," said the clerk.

"What about that one over there?" asked Roy, pointing to the unit which the man had returned.

"That one doesn't work. A fellow just brought it back."

"I'm pretty good at repairing those things," said my brother-in-law. "How much will you take for it as is?"

"Well . . . how about $20?" said the clerk.

"Right," said Roy. "Tax included."

"Right," said the clerk.

It's called outwitting or beating the system, and I suspect that Americans are really much better at it than Canadians, and certain Kentuckians may have the edge over other Americans. They have a long tradition which goes back to the first conversion of corn into a liquid asset. Although I did know one Canadian, a big, jovial man called Warren, who had a few good cracks at it. Among other things he used to sell Christmas trees. One year he brought a selection of trees to the home of a well-heeled, older resident of our town, but he could not make a sale.

"Family coming home this year," the older man explained. "I want a perfectly shaped Norway spruce, just like those ones in my yard out back."

An hour or so later Warren was at the front door again with a perfectly shaped Norway spruce, and he sold it immediately. He even got a two-dollar tip. It was not until the following spring that the man who bought the tree was walking behind his house and noticed that one of his own spruces had been cut six inches above the ground. By then Warren was somewhere out west. He seldom stays long in any one place, I gather.

Personally, however, I'm not much good at buying and selling. I brought home a picnic table this summer, bragging that the $26.95 price was not much more than the cost of the wood. The next week the same tables were on sale for $16.00. When I visited Ensenada, Mexico, a bright-eyed, angelic-looking boy about ten years old, hawking his wares on the sidewalk outside a store, gave me a "number one bargain" of a genuine leather belt, skilfully engraved, for six dollars. Inside the store, I discovered two minutes later, my wife was buying identical belts for three dollars apiece.

I suppose that I'm simply too naive, trusting and lazy to become a proper wheeler-dealer. But I did learn the other day that some coins are worth thousands of dollars, notably the 1943 Lincoln cent in copper rather than steel and the 1936 Canadian cent with a dot, which was minted temporarily then recalled when George VI became King after the sudden abdication of Edward VIII so that he could marry his American sweetheart.

One of these days, as I tried to explain to my American spouse, I'm bound to find a fortune in the penny jar.

Cheating an Honest Man

There is no longer any truth to the old saying that you can't cheat an honest man. These days honest men are like sitting ducks. Life has simply become too complicated, the cheaters too sophisticated, and there may be no such thing as absolute honesty in any case.

I learned to be honest the hard way. When I was a small boy, being raised by a staunch Presbyterian aunt who also had the girth of a heavyweight wrestler, I once cleverly slipped into my pocket a two-cent eraser from the "Five and Ten Cent Store." I must have been quite proud of my little shop-lifting foray, because when I got home I took the eraser out of my pocket and showed it off to my aunt. The next thing I knew I was heading back to the department store, this time with Aunt Janet gripping one of my wrists and my feet not touching the ground.

To my profound shame, I had to return the eraser and apologize to the manager, who, presumably satisfied with the quick restitution and the genuineness of my tearful contrition, decided not to press charges. But my wrist hurt the whole rest of the day, and for years I believed that the principle of honesty could not be bent in any way.

As I grew older, however, I discovered that even my aunt was not absolutely honest. She must have known that not all the chunks of coal I brought back from the dock yards had fallen off the railway wagons, but the coal kept the flat warm, and it didn't seem to bother her a bit. She no doubt shared the common attitude among the working classes that

119

ripping off the system whenever possible had nothing to do with honesty.

Then there was the whole area of human relations. Could you tell a neighbour that her new hairdo was a mess? Could you state bluntly to a gracious hostess who had spent hours in her kitchen that you couldn't stand baked fish and asparagus?

When I was finishing high school, a friend of mine gave me a lovely typewriter and a typing manual, explaining that once I mastered the machine I was sure to get higher marks for written assignments. He was working for a typewriter company at the time, and he also explained that the machine was a trade-in which he had gotten for nothing and had reconditioned himself.

Well, like Aunt Janet with the coal, I knew there was something not right about the windfall, but I was anxious to get those higher marks. And I actually did get higher marks, until two cops arrived at the door with a list of serial numbers and took away my by-then beloved typewriter.

During the working years that followed, I seldom thought about honesty. Garages, television repair shops, used-car dealers, mail-order firms, vending machines, the income tax people, door-to-door salesmen and a Russian watch company from which I ordered what appeared to be a bargain silver pocket watch (and which ran for exactly one hour)—they all cheated me on various occasions. The winners in our society, I soon learned, are those who know how to manipulate the system. After all, several hundred people earning more than $500,000 a year pay no income tax at all. Retired politicians and civil servants long before the age of 65 spend their winters in Florida on pensions often larger than the salaries earned by the rest of us who still plod to work.

I've tried to learn how to manipulate the system, and I've studied the methods of an expert, my Kentucky-born brother-in-law Roy. As I've mentioned already, he buys, sells, and trades guns and anything else he can get his hands on, and in the course of a year he amasses a fair piece of change, under-the-table naturally.

Roy still has a hillbilly accent, which he uses to great advantage. Not long ago, for instance, at a gun show in Chicago, another trader laughed at him and made a remark about "dumb hillbillies." Roy simply grinned foolishly, confirming the other man's prejudiced views. A few days before the next gun show in Chicago, however, Roy happened to pick up a near-perfect replica of a classic long rifle for $150. The replica is worth about $250, apparently, but a true original $2,500 or more. The day before the show, Roy took the rifle over to his father's house and asked if he could leave it overnight in the basement. His father couldn't understand why Roy wanted to do that, but he didn't object. At the show the following morning, the trader who had made the remark about "dumb hillbillies" sauntered over to Roy's display and immediately spotted the replica of the classic rifle.

"Hey, man, where'd yuh get that?" he asked.

"Found it in my pa's basement," Roy replied.

"Any idea what it's worth?"

"Well, I don't rightly know. Not a whole lot, I reckon."

"Tell you what—I'll give yuh $500."

"That don't seem right to me."

"Okay, make it $750. Cash. I got a client lookin' for one of those. Otherwise, I wouldn't give it a second glance."

"Do you really figure that's what it's worth?"

The other trader, of course, knew exactly what it was worth—$2,500 or more. The original rifle, that is.

"Naw, it ain't worth much. But this client's an old friend of mine. Look, here's $1,000 cash. Take it or leave it."

"Well, if you say so," said Roy. "Wouldn't want you to disappoint an old pal."

Three weeks later, at the same gun show, the man who bought the rifle came over to Roy in a fury. "You rotten, no-good, low-down swindler!" he shouted. "That gun you sold me was a lousy replica!"

"I tried to tell you that," replied Roy, grinning.

Over the years he has tried to smarten me up too, but I can't seem to get the hang of it. Takes me all my time just to avoid being burned too badly. I can easily do the bit about being dumb and naive, but in my case the impression is unfortunately an honest one. Probably it has something to do with a two-cent eraser.

Country Fairs

Relatively speaking, there's nothing a big city can offer that is quite like a country fair. What I mean is that in a metropolis such as Montreal or New York there are important and exciting events taking place all the time—concerts and shows, movies, big stars, bank robberies, fires, muggings, murders, riots. Small towns can't hope to match these day-to-day spectacles.

The most you get in a small town is Jack's car parked overnight in the widow Murphy's driveway again, or the Sears truck pulling up to the Mercier place to make another delivery. New sofa this time. Where do they get the money, those Merciers? Not much wrong with the old sofa either.

Relatively speaking, then, when a small city or town has its annual fair, it's the most exciting time of the year. There is 100 per cent participation. They come from the chateaux and the shacks. Some pull up in new Lincoln Continentals, and others arrive in old pickup trucks smelling of manure, half a dozen kids hanging onto the sides of the open back.

In the Eastern Townships of Quebec there are fairs in many of the small towns, but the major gathering is the Sherbrooke Exhibition, which is the same as the others except on a larger scale. There are more dare-devil acrobats and motorcyclists, more hair-raising rides, more big-name Quebec singers and comedians, more buxom country girls leading prize animals around the ring. And perhaps that's the trouble with country fairs—the animals. Personally I think that it might be better to lead the girls around the ring and leave the animals back in their barns or pens or kennels or whatever they are. You see, I had an unfortunate experience.

When I was a boy I learned to play the bagpipe, and as a result I'm occasionally in demand for weddings, Remembrance Day parades, funerals, Robert Burns suppers and happenings of the sort. Well, an official from the Sherbrooke Exhibition once called to ask me to play for the cattle display. Being city-born and raised, I used to associate the word cattle with rural serenity— herds chewing their cud in lush green fields, pails of frothing milk, tails swishing away flies, sunshine, peace, everything healthy, pure and good.

When the official told me that free tickets for all of my five kids would be thrown in, I quickly agreed to play for the cattle display. I wore my red kilt for the occasion, and I was instructed to "march around the arena, then step to the side and keep on playing until all the herds have circled and been led out."

It sounded simple enough, although I had a moment of apprehension as I struck up my pipes and out of the corner of my eye happened to notice that coming through the gate was not a rosy-cheeked country girl but a brawny man, the sinews of his arms quivering as he struggled with a metal ring. I decided to ignore that and kept my eyes straight ahead as I marched around the arena.

It was when I stepped to the side to let the parade of prize specimens pass by that I grasped the full, sinister implications of it all. I suppose I'd been conditioned by pictures of toreadors bending down from the waist and flashing their capes. But the bulls at the Exhibition made the bullfight variety look like underfed puppy dogs. Enormous, snorting beasts with necks as thick as the motors on a jumbo jet, they looked every bit as capable of propelling a quick take-off into the skies. And what was even more disturbing, their appreciation of the music of the Great Highland Pipe did not appear to be perfect. As the lead man moved by he was holding the nose ring with both hands, straining with all his might to control the monstrous animal which rolled its bulging eyes in my direction. I backed up against the arena fence and formulated contingency plans to leap over it in one bound, kilt and modesty notwithstanding.

When the parade was finished and I was standing in the arena among the assorted droppings, marvelling that I had survived without injury or worse, the Exhibition official appeared, congratulated me, and asked me about coming back the following night. "Those were just the dairy cattle tonight," he said. "Tomorrow night we have the beef cattle. They're much bigger and heftier."

Well, that did it. I've always preferred my beef well done with a mushroom sauce. The following night the Sherbrooke Exhibition was obliged to use piped-in rather than bagpipe music for the parade of the beef cattle.

But I still say there's nothing quite like a country fair.

Plumbing on the Side

I was having a formal dinner with the president and dignitaries of the university, after I had delivered a scholarly address, and the conversation touched upon many of the intricate aspects of contemporary culture and letters. Then the president asked me if I was staying over in the university's hospitality suite, and without thinking I replied, "No. I have to rush off to put in a toilet for a friend of mine."

"A what?" asked the president, eyebrows ascending.

"A toilet. This friend of mine, Alfie Epstein, is building a second bathroom. We'll be hooking up his sink and bathtub as well."

"I see," said the president. But he still looked a bit baffled, and it occurred to me that the subject was perhaps indelicate for an elegant dinner table.

Nevertheless, even if I say so myself, I am a very good plumber, probably because of my genetic make-up. From a long line of Italian tradesmen on one side, I have arms suitable for pipe wrenches and a tradition of water management which goes back to the Roman aqueducts and the tiled baths where senators recovered after orgies. From my Scottish side, I inherited the stubborn determination required to cope with rust-encrusted joints and the practical sense not to want to pay somebody $150 or so an hour to do something I can do myself.

I began plumbing out of necessity, having five small children at a time when plastic toys were all the rage. And as every parent knows, kids are born with an irresistible compulsion to flush things down toilets. They think it's magic. Or something. Occasionally a plunger will solve the problem, or the flexible wire device with a hook at the end called a plumber's snake, but there are some toys—indestructible and designed quite likely by people on the payroll of the plumbers' union—which will become wedged in the entrails of the toilet, and the only way to get them out is to dismantle the whole damned thing.

Or worse, especially in houses with old cast-iron pipes, the toy will squeeze through the toilet and get stuck in an elbow further along the plumbing system, usually where a floor, ceiling or wall has to be torn apart to get at it. Before plastics, it was possible to use the neighbour's facilities and wait for whatever was blocking the pipe to rot away. Now it's either fix it or nail shut the bathroom door.

When I taught in England for a year, my children ranged from the terrible twos to the nasty nines, and naturally, within a few days the toilet of our rented house was blocked. It was then that I discovered that the English do not expect people to do anything for themselves. I rushed desperately from one hardware store to another, but I could not buy a plunger. The clerks seemed astonished that anyone but a qualified plumber would know how to use what surely must be the simplest device since the caveman's club, and the plumbers themselves must have had a secret supply system.

But the challenge only increased my determination. No wonder Great Britain was going down the drain, I thought. Cursing to myself as I walked past a toy store, I was about to go in and denounce the whole degenerate industry when I spotted an inflatable beach ball. It worked perfectly. Pressing it down over the hole in the toilet bowl, then pulling it back up sharply, I dislodged a plastic boat and two dolls, and with a melodious "whoosh" the waters flowed again.

Plumbing, incidentally, is one of the most conservative of human enterprises. Until a few years ago, there had been no significant advances, apart from Thomas Crapper's flush system, since the ancient Babylonians, who may well have had better sewage systems than we have today.

At a conference in Trois-Rivières recently, I gave another scholarly address, then I left early so that I could fix the toilet of a former student who now teaches at l'Université du Québec. It was a tough job, the old toilet having been installed 50 years ago. But to the profound relief of my hostess, I managed eventually to get it going, and I felt quite pleased with myself.

That, I suppose, is the beautiful thing about plumbing. When I give a lecture or write a book, I have no idea what the reaction will be, and I have to brace myself for negative comments and scathing reviews. But when I fix a toilet, I can always count on a flush of sincere appreciation.

Double Windows

My neighbour has been at it all day, wrestling with his double windows, or storm windows as they are often called now, and I can't help smiling as I watch. Although I must admit that my feelings are mixed. I had the good judgement to get rid of my old double windows and install permanent, completely sealed aluminum ones, so that all I have to do is stroll around the house and close them when the arctic blasts start rattling the panes.

Previously I used to go through torment every autumn, dragging the heavy, wood-framed windows out of storage, cleaning them, putting in new putty where it had fallen out, deciding whether to tape the cracks or replace the glass. Once, when I was 20 feet or so up a ladder, hanging onto a bedroom window with one hand and trying to adjust a retainer hook with the other, I leaned back too far. The next thing I knew, the ladder was wobbling at the vertical position, and my knees were playing a drum tattoo against the rungs. I saved my neck by swinging the window towards the house, persuading the ladder to incline back against the wall.

But I lost my grip on the window, and at that very moment I made the decision to replace what was left of it and all the other wretched double windows with permanent ones.

I've never regretted that decision. In fact, if I had made it a few years earlier, the summer before the rock smashed through six window panes to be precise, I would now be able to enjoy thoroughly watching my neighbour work.

My three nephews were visiting at the time, and the six windows were stacked against the wall waiting to be washed. The two older boys were becoming quite civilized by then, but the youngest, Keith, no doubt because he always had to compete for attention, was constantly in trouble. I was taking a coffee break when I heard the resounding crash. Rushing out the door, I saw immediately that a stone had been thrown through the panes of all six windows, and there stood little Keith, all by himself, holding another stone in his hand.

He protested his innocence naturally, but I had heard such stories too many times. I was looking at a whole day's repair work and quite a few dollars' worth of new glass. You just couldn't let a youngster get away with something like that. He might grow up to be a psychopath or a protest marcher or something. Without hesitation and in great fury I did what I had to do— I grabbed the small boy and swung him over my knee. The other two boys came back in time to witness the end of the spanking, to voice their approval that the punishment fitted the terrible deed with an impressive show of self-righteousness, and to help me clean up the shattered glass while their little brother ran off howling.

Keith is married now with three children of his own, pursuing a career as a physical education instructor. His two older brothers also have wives and children, and I saw a lot of one of them when I was in Calgary a couple of years ago. Barry's a policeman now and quite often he would drop over for a coffee or a beer after a shift.

When it happened that the shift had been par- ticularly harrowing—assaults, rapes, assorted

brutalities—he would often calm himself by reminiscing about the "good old days" when he and his
brothers used to come out to my house in the country
during vacations.

He was doing exactly that one night when
suddenly he interrupted himself, looked over at me
sheepishly and announced, "You know, Uncle Ron,
I've got a confession to make."

"A what?" I asked.

"A confession. It's been on my mind all these
years."

"What on earth are you talking about?"

"You remember those six double windows that
were stacked against the wall and the rock that got
thrown through them?"

"How could I forget?"

"Well, I think you should know that Keith never
threw that rock. He could hardly have even lifted it
then."

"You don't mean . . ."

"Yes. I was the one who broke those windows."

And that is the reason that double windows have
double significance for me. They reassure me that
occasionally I can exercise good judgement, but they
also remind me that now and again I am capable of
awful blunders.

Vacation Houses

Thinking about vacations, either past or to come, is generally a pleasant experience. A vacation means escape from the routine of the working world for a few days at least, a change in surroundings, perhaps a stay in the country with the day beginning by the reassuring crow of a rooster rather than the piercing screech of an alarm clock.

For many people, I presume, vacation means renting a cottage, an experience my wife, Jean, and I lived through several times over the years. And travelling with five children, in the interests of practicality and sanity, we usually had to rent in advance, sight unseen. There was no way to take a chance on not finding accommodations and the seven of us having to sleep in the station wagon. On several trips I did bring along a large tent in the cartop carrier, but it was never used a single time. After driving all day with five kids bursting with undepleted energy, Jean and I never had the courage to tackle the tent. We settled for a motel with no surprises.

The last vacation house we rented was on one of the Florida Keys, surrounded by the tranquillizing soft greens and blues of the sea, palm trees, exotic flowers, warm Caribbean breezes scented with spice and just the hint of decaying seaweed, pelicans and egrets gliding in the blue sky over our heads, our living room the whole outdoors. It was close to paradise really, until the floor in the kitchen started to grow.

My wife, who used to spend a lot of time in kitchens, noticed it first. "My God!" she shouted. "There's something moving under the floor!" I rushed in to find her pointing, or rather trying to point to a spot where the linoleum had risen into a hump about an inch high. I stepped on the hump and it responded slightly. There was a spongy resilience, almost as if . . . then right before our eyes, another hump slowly rose. This time I jumped up and down on both of them, and Jean, a calm, resourceful woman under trying circumstances, started whacking them with a broom.

Now I knew that the kitchen had just been added to the house we were renting. The contractor's sign complete with telephone number was still in the yard, so I gave him a call. He muttered something about being very busy and said that he would be over to take care of the problem as soon as he could.

"Nothing to worry about," I assured my wife, who was now standing in the doorway staring transfixed at a third hump pushing its way into our lives, "you can just step around them when you're fixing dinner."

"We're going out for dinner," she replied.

I tried to explain to her and the kids, at the table of a modest restaurant, about underflooring and expansion and drying and curing, but I could not prevent bizarre thoughts from creeping into my own mind. After all, being a northerner, I'm more accustomed to pipes freezing and furnaces breaking down. There are some disquieting things about warm climates, like giant scorpions, hurricanes, pirates' curses and Bermuda triangles.

"I wonder if any of that contractor's relatives have disappeared lately," Jean mumbled. She got her schooling in a small one-room schoolhouse in a backward, rural area of the Kentucky hills where pupils were forced to read the short stories of Edgar Allan Poe like "The Tell-tale Heart."

To cheer her up I reminded her of all the challenges of rented houses we had successfully handled over the years. Such as the time in England when our nine-year-old daughter pushed over the china cabinet in the dining room. The resounding crash reverberated through the house, then our daughter rushed to us in the next room, mercifully unscathed. Besides shattered crystal and dishes spread wall to wall, we got to the dining room just in time to witness the last dribble from a broken bottle of cognac, which we had stowed away for such emergencies.

But over the next three lean months, for 176 pounds sterling and a few pence, we managed to replace every item which had been destroyed.

Then there was the rattling sound in the house in Scotland, caused by the slate shingles on the roof lifting in gale-force winds. The rats and flying cockroaches in Detroit. The hole in the bedroom wall of the apartment in Calgary. The six-foot-high brick wall which the neighbour built between his front walk and ours to keep our three-year-old son from trespassing on his tricycle.

The cottage we rented a few years ago on one of the remote out-islands of the Bahamas was advertised as having three bedrooms, "incidentals not included." One of the bedrooms turned out to be a clothes closet, and after my four daughters had washed their hair a few times—I tried to offset the shampoo ads by explaining that it was unhealthy to remove the natural oils, but to no avail—we found out about the "incidentals."

When no water would come out of the taps, I presumed that something had gone wrong with the plumbing and strolled over to see the real estate agent, as he called himself.

"Your reservoir is empty," he announced matter-of-factly. "You can order some more water, if you like. They bring it over by barge."

It cost six cents a gallon, and when I checked the reservoir under the porch after the men had filled it with a long hose from the barge, I could swear that I saw frogs and various other unidentifiable aquatic creatures swimming around in it.

In Florida, our sojourn came to an end with no sign of the contractor other than the one standing in the yard. The first hump appeared to have shrunk slightly, but a fourth had surfaced under the table. By then, however, we had all learned to live with them.

Not often, I imagine, does anything in life come up to our full expectations. But that doesn't matter— simply to have expectations is what makes life worth living. It would take a lot more than a few bumps in a floor to diminish the joyful thought of a vacation.

Year of the Roses

My roses have reached new heights of magnificence this year. Two pink blossoms on one bush are a full six inches across, several other bushes have more than a dozen red, yellow or white flowers each, and new buds are forming every day.

It is even more impressive than the year I planted what were labelled "dwarf nasturtiums" among the morning glories in front of the veranda. They ascended past the railing, up the posts, along the edge of the roof and back down, 20 feet at least. Unfortunately that never happened again, and my morning glories, probably traumatized, have never been quite the same either.

People often ask how I tend my spectacular rose garden, and in order not to appear ridiculous I usually mutter something about mulch and bone meal, but the truth is that I do very little. The rose bushes were there when I bought my old house in the country, and each spring, if I get the chance, I simply add a couple more.

My knowledge of gardening is minimal. Where I was born and raised in the tenement district of a big city, there were no rose gardens. In fact, what grass there was pushed up through cracks in the pavement. Grass is perverse that way, I've learned. To restore a patch in the lawn you can dig six inches deep, put in the best top soil, add peat moss and fertilizer, spread the highest grade of seed, water regularly, and not a blade of grass will grow. Yet the damned stuff will push up through cracks in the pavement.

At the age of nine or ten, I bought two little packages of seeds, hollyhocks and chrysanthemums, with my paper-route money and planted them, along with potatoes, in a vacant lot not far from our flat. But the flowers never grew, and I wrote them off, telling myself that flowers were something mainly associated with funeral parlours in any case. The potatoes, however, seemed to flourish, until the time came to dig them up, and I discovered that every single one of them was riddled with worm holes.

I have to admit that I've come a long way from the city streets and back lanes where I grew up during the Great Depression and World War years. For myself and many others I knew in those days, despite the fact that the world in general is locked into a series of disasters, there have been undeniable improvements.

Listening to my five teenagers alternate hour-long conversations on the telephone, then moaning over the phone bills, I remember the times when my aunt took sick and I had to run 10 or 12 blocks to the doctor's office or a relative's home because we had no telephone then. Neither did we have hot water or an electric refrigerator, not to mention such unthinkable luxuries as washers and dryers.

Dental problems used to be solved by going to the teaching clinic and having all your teeth pulled out. Sickness or accidents had to be extreme before anyone considered seeing a doctor. My left arm has been crooked since I was about 13 years old. The gang on my block was playing football in the street against a rival gang. It was decided that since I was the smallest kid in the game, I should carry the ball as a strategy to fool the other team, the big guys blocking for me.

Well, the other team wasn't fooled and the big guys didn't do much blocking. Two weeks later, when the swelling and pain in my elbow had not responded to the usual compresses and poultices, I was hauled to the out-patients' clinic of the old Montreal General Hospital, located then below Ste. Catherine Street off St. Lawrence Boulevard. The X-ray showed a small bone broken in the elbow, and I got to wear a cast that all my friends could scribble on, but it was too late to set the bone properly.

That wasn't too bad, I suppose, comparatively speaking. I can remember whole families of a dozen or more children who were all grotesquely bow-legged because of rickets, the disease which results from vitamin deficiency, chiefly the lack of milk. Polio and TB were common afflictions in those days. Annual medical checkups were unheard of in the working-class districts. There can be no doubt that the quality of life for the average individual has defi-nitely gotten better over the past 40 years or so. But my five children cannot fully appreciate the fact. They have greater sophistication than either my wife or I could ever muster. Lately they have been hounding me to dig up my roses and install a swim-ming pool. They get a lot of the things they ask for, I'm afraid, but there is no way they'll get the swim-ming pool.

"You never promised me a rose garden," my wife said jokingly one day when I called her out to see the latest blossoms.

And she was right. Being of reasonably sound mind and body, except for a slightly crooked arm, and never having believed that the world owed me anything, I made no promises. I just plodded along as best I could. And we got lucky, I guess.

The Season of the Hunter

I never imagined that I would find myself in the bush
at dusk with my thumb twitching on the safety catch
of a rifle, shivering in the freezing rain, staring into
expanding pools of darkness and turning my head
every few moments to check on my son.

For most of us who live in rural areas, it must be
said, hunting season is not greeted with joy. The
woods are suddenly festering with thousands of
desperadoes, all of them with powerful weapons and
too many of them braced by a bellyful of booze.
Anything that moves in the bush or fields is in
danger—cows, horses, dogs, people. Two residents of
my own village in the Eastern Townships of Quebec
have been shot dead by hunters. And, of course, each
year a few hunters succeed in killing themselves or
each other.

I have heard all the arguments—culling the deer
population to prevent starvation, fostering the skills
necessary in the event of war, preserving traditional
rights and freedoms. Native peoples in the North, a
few others perhaps, hunt because they need and want
the meat. But most hunters today undoubtedly pay
more for equipment and travel than the cost of whatever food they may bring home, if they bother to
bring it home at all.

Why, then, was I waiting in the bush? Well, I keep
four beehives at the edge of a wood behind my house,
and usually I can count on harvesting between 400
and 700 pounds of honey each season. After taking
off the honey in the autumn, I make sure the bees
have enough food to last them the winter, then I put

Styrofoam huts of my own design over the hives to protect them from the cold. If I say so myself, I am a good beekeeper. A man needs to believe that he can do at least something productive.

When I wandered up to my little apiary for a routine inspection, to my consternation I discovered that one hive had been literally torn apart. The supers—wooden boxes to hold the frames on which the bees build their wax comb—were on their sides. The frames themselves had been knocked out of the supers and were scattered about in pieces. Honey, wax, bees, brood, even the wires to hold the combs straight had been devoured.

Damned raccoons, I thought—life in the country is a running battle of wits with raccoons— and I rushed back to get my son. We wrapped heavy wire around the remaining three hives and placed large boulders on top of the covers. "That'll do it," I said. "No raccoon will ever get into those hives now."

First thing the following morning we headed right up to the hives. Standing stupefied in the dawn sunlight, my son and I witnessed a scene of nearly total devastation. The boulders had been flicked aside as if they were pebbles. The wires had been snapped like pieces of thread. Pitiful handfuls of bees clustered around the remnants of supers and frames spread over a radius of several yards. One hive, miraculously, was intact.

In a state of unthinking fury I grabbed a stick and started along the trail which had been clearly beaten through the bush. It was my son who brought me to my senses.

"Look, Dad," he said, pointing down. They were unmistakable—tracks sunk a good six inches into the soft ground, as large around as fence posts. There was a lingering odour. We decided to retreat.

"Lot of bears around this year," said the Game Warden over the phone. "Sounds like that 400-pound giant a guy reported last week."

"Can you come out with one of those tranquillizer guns and take him away?" I asked.

"We don't do that around here," he replied, seemingly amused.

"Then what am I supposed to do?"

"Go ahead and shoot it."

The bee inspector was more explicit. "If you don't shoot it," he said, "it'll keep coming back. Nothing else for it."

"But I'm not a hunter."

"Spread the word. There are hundreds of guys who'll be more than happy to get rid of it for you."

Now the last thing I wanted was a hundred rabid hunters with high-powered rifles prowling the bush a few yards from my house. "We can shoot 'im ourselves," said my son. "Please, Dad," he added.

I knew that he was right. The responsibility to deal with the marauding bear was ours alone.

So we waited, upwind, listening for the tell-tale crack of a branch, probing the lengthening shadows for the shape of the great furry beast which could slap around beehives as if they were matchboxes. Seven nights we waited, nerves steeled, determined to get that bear.

But I guess three hives were enough. Or else he knew that we were there. Anyway, he did not come back.

"Too bad," said my strapping son, genuinely disappointed.

Myself, I was not sorry. My anger was spent. The bear had merely done his thing. The silent, twilight vigils had given me a lot of time to explore the shadowed regions of my own mind, and I did not always like what I found.

I know now that hunting is not a sport—it is the release of a primitive savagery which lurks in the basic nature of human beings. My bear came out on top. But now that the twitching trigger finger can be on the release button of a nuclear bomb instead of a rifle, neither we nor the bears may have much hope of winning.

Clothes and the Man

My four daughters, and even occasionally my son, are constantly telling me how to dress.

"You look like an absolute slob, Dad," one of them will gently remark, and another will add, "Would you do us a big favour and throw those pants and that shirt out in the garbage. I've got a friend coming over. How do you think I feel with my father wearing awful things like that?"

Probably they are right. I admit that I am not very clothes conscious. I might have been perhaps, if my older cousin had not been built so much shorter and stockier than I was as a boy. In those Depression days when eating was the sole priority, he was the main source of the hand-me-downs I used to wear, and no amount of alteration seemed to achieve a proper fit. Consequently, I didn't spend time worrying about how I looked, which in any case was about the same as most of the other kids on the block.

Later, when I became a college student, I actually bought a suit, at a sale in Eaton's bargain basement. It was charcoal grey and fit perfectly, and by never sitting down or bending my arms when I had it on, I managed to make it last until I had completed three degrees and had become a university lecturer myself. The end came shamefully. I was writing something on the blackboard and dropped the chalk. As I bent down I could hear the sound of cloth deteriorating, more of a quiet, expiring rasp than an actual rip. I had to sidle like a crab over to the classroom door and back out, while the students stared with various degrees of wonder.

In my office I somehow managed to get the pieces to hold together with paper clips and staples, but when I got home that night, my wife, an expert with a sewing machine, explained that the material was simply too thin to repair. I had, however, at least gotten my money's worth out of that suit. To this day I still grieve about what happened to my elegant brown slacks, which I splurged on to save wearing the suit while I was a graduate student in Detroit.

I was so fond of those stylish slacks that every so often I used to take them to a dry-cleaners near where I was living. Then one day when I went to pick them up, the door to the place was chained and padlocked. The policeman who was standing there explained to me that the store had been a front for a bookie operation and had been raided.

I looked in the store window, and right there in plain view I could see my brown slacks hanging on a rack, all cleaned and neatly pressed.

"Do you think you could open the door for ten seconds and let me grab my pants?" I pleaded with the cop. He shook his head.

"Those are my best pants. They're mine. They belong to me," I protested, but to no avail. Apparently I would have to wait until the case came up in court, whereupon I could send in a claim in triplicate along with proof of ownership. For three months I walked past that store and had to gaze at my beautiful slacks in the window. Then the semester came to an end, I went back to Montreal, and I never laid eyes on them again.

During the early years of marriage and five children in fairly rapid succession, I was too busy dealing with diapers, dolls and indestructible plastic toys blocking the toilet to think about clothes. I simply replaced what my wife insisted was worn out and tried to look more or less like most other people. When my daughters, the same young ladies who are so sensitive about what I wear in my own house, got to be teenagers, I discovered that they had no compunctions about making off with any half-decent garment I had, including shirts, sweaters, jackets and the treasured white cowboy hat presented to me for making a speech in Calgary. My son, who at age 14 had feet three sizes larger than mine, went for my socks. Pressed for time, on more than one occasion I have in fact been reduced to wearing two odd socks and loosening my belt so that my pants would hang low.

The truth is, however, that I admire and envy smartly dressed people. Good appearance is important—it can land you a job, win you an election, attract a sweetheart, get you a seat in a restaurant. But I can't help recalling how I used to envy my brother-in-law's wavy, perfectly controlled hair, a contrast to my own unruly shock. Well, he's bald now, and I still have a full head of hair.

I try to explain to my children that if I look a bit sloppy at times, it's because I never had the opportunity to acquire discrimination and taste. Besides, if Fate had wanted me to be a natty dresser, then my cousin would have been taller, slimmer and richer, and the Detroit fuzz would never have busted that bookie joint.

Back to School

School opening comes as a relief to many parents, I suppose, but for my wife and myself, who through some form of madness had five children in six years, it is a time of frenzy and often despair.

When my four girls and their younger brother were all going to the same small-town elementary school, the problems mainly had to do with clothing and human relations. One would absolutely refuse to stay in the same room with a certain teacher or classmate, another could not possibly survive the day separated from a special friend. Annually I went into debt buying pencils, erasers, notebooks, shoes, gym shorts, dresses, sweaters and sundry other items such as skate boards or fancy T-shirts, which, I was solemnly assured, all the other kids had and without which there could be no reason to continue living.

Each school morning my wife and I did our imitation of the United Nations peacekeeping force, trying to prevent the girls from making off with each other's clothes or from homicidal retaliation when the attempt succeeded.

Actually, now that my daughters are supposedly mature young women, the clothes snatching, if anything, has gotten worse, the only mitigating factor being that they spread it out a little by also grabbing whatever they fancy from both my wife's and my own diminishing wardrobes. And, of course, it is no longer a few dollars for pencils and erasers. My son has already explained to me that if he is to play for the school hockey team and not have his career totally thwarted, then I will have to buy him a pair of skates with moulded boots and stainless steel blades or something, at a cost in the $150 range. Not to mention the new helmet, gauntlets, pads . . . I told him how I used to stuff old newspapers down my socks when I played hockey. His reply was that I, obviously an unfeeling brute and unfit parent, was willing to risk having my son injured, in fact just about forcing him to be crippled, no doubt permanently.

My four daughters now attending college think of only one thing besides "handsome hunks." Since I have not rushed out to buy them all their own cars, I must bear the heavy responsibility of crushing their personalities, spoiling their appetites, ruining their chances to achieve self-realization, reducing them to such a state of utter deprivation that they can no longer face their mobile peers.

In view of the energy crisis, they do not insist on a big car. They could force themselves to make do with some little thing . . . like an MG or a TR or a Porsche.

If I am too stingy to buy each one her own car, my four daughters say, then they would be willing to settle for a "family" automobile. All four will share it equally, they assure me, liberating my wife and me from the burden of taxi service, transporting them-selves to seventh heaven and fullness of life hitherto evident only on television.

"Yeah . . . just like you 'share' your socks, blouses and blue jeans," I reply sneeringly. Then I tell them that I will buy a second car as soon as one is manufactured which will go in four directions at the same time. One has to be clever to deal with these situations.

I am still trying to find an equally disarming response for my son, who can be infuriatingly advanced for his age and whose imagination has a tendency to soar out of control. He has his sights set on a helicopter, or a motorcycle and a small hovercraft.

For pupils in Quebec small towns, transportation to and from school, I admit, can be a problem. Ever since the Ministry of Education and the Regional School Boards in their infinite wisdom decided to replace local high schools with giant comprehensive factories, my children and thousands of others have spent one to three hours a day on buses.

Losing the local combination elementary and high schools also dealt a blow to community spirit and identity, for the schools traditionally served for dances, sports, meetings and various other village functions. For me, therefore, school opening means not only frenzy and despair, but lingering anger at bureaucratic idiocy. I wrote letters, prepared petitions and did everything I could to prevent the conversion to huge, impersonal comprehensive schools, pointing out that many areas of the United States were abandoning them in favour of mobile labs and other alternatives.

With a little luck, however, in two or three years' time my youngest will be through junior college and I won't have to think about schools any more. By then, I suppose, he'll want a Learjet so that he can commute to university in Miami and cultivate a suntan.

Reverse Gear

In the last few years I have often wondered whether the world around me is going backwards or forwards.

I once swore that I would never do it, certainly not without the aid of a team of sly, sharp-eyed experts each of whom was either a reliable member of the family or owed me something, but last week there I was—in a used-car lot. A plain case of blackmail, of course. My two oldest daughters, egged on by my other three teenagers, have explained to me in sobering tones that without cars of their own there can be no possible reason to continue living.

We reside in a tiny, apparently dumb country village in the Eastern Townships of Quebec, by a dumb lake, with nothing but pure mountain air, fresh garden produce, eggs warm from the farm, swimming, boating, water-skiing, fishing and cross-country skiing to offset the horror of isolation from the real world. The weekends are especially hard to bear, because the town is crowded with so many silly tourists who come to gawk at the scenery.

As I've mentioned before, my daughters have been telling me every night at the dinner table that not having their own cars, their social life is a pitiful disaster, their personalities are being deformed, their intellects are withering away from under-stimulation, their complexions are being ruined, and it is all my fault. One of them has even suggested that with parents so insensitive, stingy and stupid as my wife and myself, she must surely have been adopted or else the victim of a mix-up in the maternity ward.

149

So there I was, conned again, and about to find out that used-car lots and salesmen have not changed a great deal since I bought my first jalopy back in 1958. I was living in Detroit at the time, and I must admit that I did not do too badly, but that was only because I had been warned and had brought along a task force of Kentucky in-laws hardened by adversity and highly skilled in the tricks of the trade.

One cousin, in fact, made his living with a machine which cut treads in bald tires, making them look brand new, even though they might not last five miles. He checked the rubber that day. Another in-law, using a stick in the manner of a doctor with a stethoscope, listened to the motors.

Needless to say, we passed on more than one "best deal in the U.S. of A." Physically the car dealers were different people, but they all seemed to have the same smooth knowing attitude, the same ingratiating smile oozing with sincerity and concern, the same willingness to sacrifice for my benefit. I became more and more appalled at what would have happened if I had been alone.

Finally, after wandering miles along the motor city's Livernois Avenue, which with its car lots lining both sides of the street for as far as the eye could see was surely the Mecca of second-hand North American mobility, I bought a 1952 Ford for $200. Cash. The sum total of all the money I had at the time. It was an old clunker, but it served me well for years, until I traded it in on a new imported car, which blew its motor two weeks after the guarantee ran out.

With my daughters last week in the used-car lot, the only vehicles I saw for under $1000 were dented, rust-riddled hulks. I put my foot on the bumper of one of them and it fell off. Pushed the seat back on another and I was looking at the bare ground through a hole the size of a pie plate.

Eventually a salesman sidled over to us. He looked alarmingly familiar. "What do you have in mind?" he asked with an ingratiating toothy smile oozing with sincerity and concern.

"You wouldn't happen to have a '52 Ford?" I said as a joke.

His eyes lit up like the lights on the old pinball machines.

"I can do even better," he said. "Come with me."

It was a 1950 Ford, but it reminded me very much of my old 1952. There was a look of solidity, as if it were made of real metal. My mind meandered back to Livernois Avenue and my original $200 investment in the automobile industry.

"How much?" I asked.

"Well, now . . ." His eyes lit up again. "A fella was in here just yesterday and offered me $7000 for that beauty. Didn't know nothing about cars he didn't. Almost an insult, you might say . . ."

I stood there stunned. It's true after all, I thought, the world is going backwards, and at a pace that is driving us all mad. I have been trying to explain this phenomenon to my daughters, pointing out that the wisest thing they can do now is to ride their bicycles until we can find a used horse, which should then bide us over until we all get accustomed to walking again, with a view, of course, ultimately to crawl around on our hands and knees.

Wines News and Old

I was not standing in line when the new Beaujolais wine came on the market this year. Thinking back to the one time when I did line up to buy wine, I am reminded of the words of Robert Burns, "The best laid schemes o' mice and men gang aft agley," which in my case might be rephrased: "The best wines laid away by fathers gang aft to the gang."

It was in 1967 that I stood in line. Not that I was much of a connoisseur. The typical working-class family I was part of in the East End of Montreal ranked wine somewhere between Kik Cola and lemonade. At Christmas my aunt used to buy one gallon of the cheapest available sherry to go with the Scottish shortbread, and that was it.

I was diabolically sabotaged by that sherry once. In the midst of preparing for a university exam, I slipped into the kitchen when my aunt wasn't around and filled one of the old milk bottles with the stuff. Then I sipped away at it as I studied a textbook, and I can recall how both the book and the sherry seemed to improve as the evening progressed. But when I woke up the next morning, still fully dressed, I couldn't for the life of me remember a word I had read. I knew that I had finished the whole book, because my notes were in the margins to the last page. In fact, my comments seemed to become increasingly profound, illustrated by elaborate if somewhat squiggly diagrams, but the blackboard of my mind had been wiped clean. I had to read the whole damned book over again.

The reason I was in line in 1967 was that I had heard it was a rare, four-star year for French wines.

The oldest of my four daughters was six at the time, and somehow I got the notion that I should lay away a special bottle of wine for her wedding. By the time she got married, I speculated, the wine would be properly aged and of considerable value. Besides, at the rate I was going kid-wise, there was a fair chance that by then I might be destitute and unable to afford anything else.

While waiting in line, I chanced to strike up a conversation with an affable, French-born ex-priest, who advised me to invest in Châteauneuf du Pape. I figured that with his background he probably had inside knowledge of a beverage with a name like that. By the time I got to the counter, intoxicated by the general grapevine euphoria in the air, I had decided to blow the bundle on five bottles of wine, including one for the wedding of my year-old son. I believe the bottles cost about four or five dollars apiece.

I built my little wine cellar by soldering together a few large tomato-juice tins. After consulting encyclopaedias and various other authorities, then checking temperatures, humidity and angles, I found the most appropriate location at the back of a cupboard in the basement. My five precious bottles of Châteauneuf du Pape**** were carefully placed in the top row of the tomato-can rack, leaving room below for a few lesser vintages which I picked up on paydays from time to time. Whenever I went down to the cellar to get a bottle of wine for a festive dinner, I reached up and fondled the four-star treasures silently maturing, inconspicuously closing in on perfection in the top row. And I continued to do so for 14 years.

A few days before the marriage of my first daughter, my future son-in-law and his parents came to dinner. It was the occasion to open the first bottle of Châteauneuf du Pape****—a couple of hours before the meal so that it would have a chance to breathe and we all would have a chance to gaze at it in awe and anticipation.

We were not disappointed. It was superb—full-bodied, subtle, exquisitely delicious. My future in-laws, people of excellent taste of course, sipped slowly and beamed their delight, while I congratulated myself on my inspired foresight of 14 years past. And the other four bottles will be even better, I told myself.

The following summer my wife and I drove down to Nova Scotia for a weekend writers' conference, leaving our 17-year-old daughter and 14-year-old son to look after the house, dog, cats and bees. When we got back, we realized from the assorted debris that our children had thrown "a little party for a few of our friends." They had cleaned out all the food in the house, but that was to be expected. It was when I went down to the basement bathroom that I noticed the door to the cupboard where I had my little wine cellar was open. In the next instant, I was confronted with the full horror—all four remaining bottles of Châteauneuf du Pape**** were gone!

I raged in vain. My son and daughter swore that they did not know what had happened. Dozens of teenagers had been in and out of the house. Friends of friends of people they hardly knew had dropped by to share in the experience.

If I found out who had taken the wine, what really could I do? Even teenagers with the best part-time jobs never have enough money to pay for more than hamburgers, cassette tapes, rock concert tickets and gas. The wine was irreplaceable in any case. The saddest part, perhaps, was the thought that the culprits would no doubt have preferred Baby Duck.

I've never since had the will to lay away bottles of wine, and I am still trying to forget the whole sordid affair. Perhaps I should think seriously about investing in a couple of gallons of cheap sherry.

Twenty-One

It's a little sobering to have the first of your children reach her 21st birthday, especially when the country is going through another of its wretched mail strikes and your daughter is far away from home, working as an au pair with a family travelling in England, leaving her own family with meandering thoughts and memories. Where did the time go?

Surely it was only a few weeks ago that I held a tiny, five-pound, five-ounce infant in my arms, marvelling at the miracle of birth and experiencing a curious combination of ecstasy and anxiety, wanting to hug her as tightly as I could but afraid to squeeze in case I hurt such a delicate creature.

Diapers—Lord, how I hated diapers! And when my first daughter finally decided that she didn't need them any more, my wife and I had two others in diapers with two more to come. Strange how time plays tricks with our minds. It seems to me that I spent an eternity surrounded by diapers, and now that eternity seems to be encased within an interval of a few days.

We went through the usual trauma of the first day in school. With no older siblings to provide reassurance, my first daughter had to go it alone. But what a pleasant surprise at the parents' night concert for my wife and me to see with our own eyes that our own small daughter, in a pink dress with a ribbon in her hair, was by far the smartest and prettiest girl in the school.

Then there were the tough times, such as when my neighbour's son barely missed her eye with an arrow and I flew into a mindless rage, breaking the "unbreakable" fibreglass bow and arrow into little pieces in front of two innocent, uncomprehending kids. The time I left an open can of paint by the staircase I was painting to answer the phone, and she redecorated the side of our new car. And the night that she and a girlfriend managed to sneak out the back window of her room at 11 p.m. to go to a party somewhere in town. I discovered the empty room by accident, looking for a magazine, then spent two hours waiting in panic. That was when the first white hairs appeared in my black beard.

Those silver strands were soon joined by many others, strangely enough always in my beard rather than on my head. Perhaps it is because I used my jaws more than my head, grinding my teeth and raving and shouting, trying to impose my idea of order on the small world around me.

She knew, the diabolical little imp, that I would drive through a snowstorm to pick her up after she had purposefully missed the last bus home. Although I must say that even as a child she was remarkably unselfish and sharing.

At the age of 18 and legal maturity, during the year that I was invited to take the newly created Chair of Canadian Studies at the University of Calgary, she decided that she was going to strike out on her own. In the best North American tradition she would go west to seek her fortune. She arrived at my three-room apartment in Calgary, Alberta, to stay over two or three days until she found a job and suitable accommodations. Being bilingual, she was immediately hired by the Petroleum Club Restaurant, which apparently had a number of members from France.

I brought her lists of rooms and apartments from the bulletin boards of the university, but she kept putting off actually contacting anybody. When my term was over and I was leaving my apartment, I paid the rent for the rest of the month and told her that she could simply stay on there. But she was in the seat beside me and we played cribbage on the flight home from Calgary.

Yet I don't mean to imply that she is not independent. At times she's the most independent, stubborn cuss I could ever imagine, perhaps even more so than her mother, who at the age of 18 jumped on a train in Detroit and came to live with me in faraway Montreal, where I had a summer job as a newspaper reporter. I can see now that there's a lot of my wife's strength of character in my daughter. My wife was barely 21 herself when my first daughter was born.

Good God—21st birthday! *Où sont les neiges d'antan?*—where are the snows of yesteryear? Where is the little girl who used to help me herd the four younger kids to the restaurant on Sunday morning to give Mommy a well-merited break?

Because she was the oldest of five she had a lot of responsibility laid on her young shoulders, I know. She had to grow up faster than the others. But I suppose that's one of the reasons why my daughter Janet is now such a strong, capable young woman, so much like my beloved Aunt Janet, who took me in and raised me and after whom my first daughter is named.

Happy birthday, sweetheart, wherever you are.

Saying Clever Things

The pun is surely the lowest form of wit. I think of punsters as people with a diabolical streak, who will snatch a perfectly innocent word as it comes out of your mouth, twist it into some grotesque deformation of itself, then toss it into the air to amuse themselves and everybody else who happens to be around. And at your expense.

Punsters never listen to the substance of what you are trying to say. Like a cat at a mouse hole, they wait patiently, ready to pounce, occasionally twitching their tails. I should know, because I am surrounded by them—my brothers-in-law, my kids, a few of my colleagues and two virtuosos of the sport of verbal gymnastics, my mother and my wife.

When Jane Fonda launched her book on keeping in shape, for example, my wife, Jean, noted that for years in support of her various causes Miss Fonda had left "no stone unturned," but now she had decided to leave "no stern untoned." Spurred no doubt by envy of the well-preserved actress, my wife wanted to show that she could still come up with a curve or two of her own.

A little while ago, she and some friends decided to take a short-cut across a property where a priest was living. To avoid being noticed, they crept along behind some undergrowth, careful to keep a safe distance from the house, but sure enough, they rounded a clump of bushes and bumped right into the clergyman. He was reciting his breviary, and when he lifted his eyes, they were filled with the wrath of the riled righteous. But yea my good wife's tongue failed

159

her not. "Father, forgive us our trespasses," she
promptly intoned, and what could the poor preacher
do but smile and wave them on their way.

My colleague Michael Greenstein is another *bon
mot* addict, and when he starts egging on my wife, the
result is often a kind of punsters' ham session. Like
many beekeepers, I have Italian bees, which are
favoured because they are easily managed and highly
productive. When Mike phoned for me one day, my
wife told him that I was up the hill communing with
my bees.

"What language does he use?" asked Mike.

"Why, Italian of course. They're Italian bees,"
Jean quickly replied.

"I would have thought that he'd use Elizabethan
English," said Mike.

"Oh?"

"You know—to bee or not to bee."

I should mention, incidentally, that being of a
mixed family and operating in a bilingual community, I am forced to endure puns in the two tongues,
and if anything, puns in French are even worse than
those in English. The other day my brother-in-law
Jean-Guy regaled me with a story about two men
sharing a kitchen. One morning one turns to the other
angrily and says *"Tomatoes."* The other snaps back
"Potatoes," to which the first replies *"Oignon."*

Now to get that one you have to have an ear for
colloquial Quebec French. *"Tomatoes"* is *"T'as mes
toastes"*—you got my toast, and *"Potatoes"* is *"Pas
tes toastes"*—it's not your toast, and *"Oignon,"*
French for onion, comes out more or less like *"Oh
Non."* Perhaps it's just as well if you don't have an
ear for colloquial Quebec French.

When a sophisticated literary friend of mine came to visit, he told a story about driving on a bridge over a flooding stream. "Then I felt the car jolt," he said, "and I knew that I had hit something. I stopped on the other side to look, and do you know what I saw floating on the water?"

My wife and I couldn't imagine what he saw.

"A three-foot pike! I had run over a pike!"

"Must have been a turnpike," commented my wife.

My mother, naturally, has had a lot more practice than my wife. I don't dare say exactly how many, but she has been known to keep a bit of ammunition stored away in the warehouse of her brain for several decades just to have the chance to zap somebody with it once.

One time, however, when we were all having dinner together, Jean was getting the better of her. After an hour or so of verbal sparring, in desperation my mother hit below the belt. She knew that my wife, who had just refused dessert, was watching her weight.

"Expecting again?" she asked, pointedly looking Jean up and down.

"No, we finally found out what was causing them," was the sharp retort.

But my mother, rising from the table and to the occasion, got in the last word.

"My, you do say clever things," was her smiling rejoinder.

Since there is no known cure for the disease, I have learned to live with it, steeling myself whenever I see eyes light up and devilish grins form on faces. And I take special pride in the fact that I at least do not resort to hit and run with wit and pun.

Sign of the Scorpio

My daughter Katherine Rebecca and I are both Scorpios, which means that our birthdays are coming up in November. She will be turning the magic age of 21. Needless to say, I won't. Nor would I want to be 21 again, because as I think back the memories which flood into my mind are mostly of problems, pains, embarrassments, dilemmas and anxieties of every sort. For one thing, I was still recovering from a motorcycle accident, hobbling around on a mangled foot and trying to get used to a partial plate which replaced three front teeth deposited on a highway.

In a restaurant once, with a girl I was desperately trying to impress and two other couples, I forgot myself and bit into one of those delicious crusty rolls. To my utter horror, the partial plate popped out of my mouth and described an arc right into the ashtray in the middle of the table. As the others looked on bemused, momentarily holding back bursts of laughter, I snatched up my teeth and rushed into the bathroom. How I ever brought myself to return to the table, I don't know.

In fact, I was convinced that people were laughing at me much of the time—at my grotesque limp, at my uncontrollable mop of hair, at the overcoat I picked up for two dollars in a pawn shop, at the scar on my chin. Day after day in my 21st year I dragged myself on and off the old No. 3 and No. 5 streetcars, travelling back and forth from the East End to attend McGill University, where I was attempting to do a two-year MA in one year, having come to the conclusion that a small scholarship and my part-time

162

earnings were simply not enough to allow me to continue the dubious business of studying much longer.

Apart from the deep appreciation I had for a few special friends and a group of excellent professors, notably Constance Beresford-Howe, Joyce Hemlow, Louis Dudek and Hugh MacLennan, I seldom felt at ease in the McGill of those days. I was an outsider, too busy studying, travelling, working and coping to fit into the carefree student life.

The climax of my discomfort came when my partner, Gerry Charness, and I won a debate against arch-rival University of Toronto. One of the most spectacular belles on campus had been, incredibly I thought, paying particular attention to me. Presuming victory in the debate, Barbara had invited me to a celebration party just for the two of us at her posh home on the heights of the mountain. A chaffeured limousine would be waiting to take us there.

The fiasco began when the newspapers printed announcements of the big debate, and for the first time in her life, Joan, the East End girl I had been dating more or less regularly, took a notion to surprise me by attending. She was a pleasant, loving young woman really, but she had a temper, and growing up with four older brothers had endowed her with a certain toughness and a few indelicate moves. She also tended to be a bit possessive.

The audience was still cheering when the campus beauty, her long blonde hair radiantly coiffured, breathtaking in an elegant, off-the-shoulder party dress, glided backstage and threw her arms around me in something more than a congratulatory embrace.

"You were absolutely marvellous," she whispered in my ear. "I never want to let you go." My pulse quickened. Then it quickened even more as I spotted my East End girlfriend moving through the crowd towards us. As I nervously disentangled myself from Barbara, Joan stepped forward and without a moment's hesitation landed a haymaker on the other girl's jaw.

There was nothing to do but disappear as quickly as possible. I caught a glimpse of the waiting limousine as we hustled around the corner. At the age of 21 I seemed to be constantly trying to extricate myself from messes of that sort.

My daughter Kate, on the other hand, is much more organized and capable than I used to be. She even worries that at her advanced age she has not yet decided definitely what she will do with her life, and I try to explain to her that I never knew what I was going to do the next day, let alone the rest of mine. She does have a tendency to lose her cool from time to time. But since she's taking karate lessons, she'll probably be able to get by with a few menacing yells and poses rather than having to land unladylike haymakers. I'm a typically biased father, I know, but she has inherited her mother's exceptional good looks and strong will. She is also intelligent and exceedingly charming when she wants to be, and I have a strong feeling that she'll make the best of her 21st year.

But I still would not want to do it over again myself . . . Well, perhaps that's not entirely true. If miracles were possible, I might consider another go, but only on condition that I had never ridden a wretched motorcycle and that I could be 21 again knowing what I know now.

Bumps and Bombs

Headstrong is the word I would use to describe each of my five children, although on occasion I find more expressive ways to put it. And certainly they don't get the trait from me. My guardian aunt, who had a vast collection of old Scottish sayings, often used to tell me that I had a "one-track mind," but by that she meant determination and power of concentration.

At least I think that's what she meant.

With my four daughters and son, it is simply that when they get something into their heads, no matter how impractical, impossible or ridiculous, trying to talk any one of them out of it is like taking a deep breath and trying to blow away the clouds in the sky.

My third daughter, Velma, is perhaps the worst example. Just before Christmas she decided that she would go to Florida for two weeks. She had taken a semester off college and worked last winter, putting away a nice little bundle of cash. I pointed out to her how foolish and irresponsible it was to blow the whole, hard-earned bundle on a frivolous escapade.

"It's all your fault," she replied. "You're the one who taught us to love travelling."

It is true that I did take the kids on a number of trips. When the oldest was nine and the youngest two and a half, for example, I accepted an invitation to teach for a year in Great Britain. My wife and I ignored warnings about the problems of travelling with small children. After all, following her husband who was already here, my grandmother had come over from Scotland in 1907 on a tramp steamer, with eight children and pregnant with another.

With a pack on my back, a suitcase in each hand, a third under one arm and my son under the other, at Dorval Airport I must have looked like a prospector's mule heading for the Klondike. Not a porter in sight. Yet on other occasions, when travelling alone with a briefcase or a small overnight bag, I've had porters climbing over each other's backs to offer their services.

But eventually we were aboard the plane, and by mid-Atlantic my wife and five children were all sound asleep. Apart from my son deciding to take a private sight-seeing tour and being lost for three hours in the town of Bridge of Allen, then our baggage being misplaced for three weeks on a railway siding in Edinburgh during the worst part of the worst winter in Europe over 75 years, travelling within Britain was not too bad.

Preparing to return to Canada, however, having exhausted our budget to replace the dishes smashed when one of my daughters pulled over the china cabinet in the house we were renting, the best deal I could get was with the Irish airline Aer Lingus. Then the day before departure, our bags all packed and ready to be hauled, I picked up a newspaper to read that the IRA, for reasons I never quite grasped, was threatening to blow all Aer Lingus planes out of the sky. My wife and I were stunned. We couldn't imagine what on earth the IRA could have against us. The children were laughing and shouting and play-fully banging around the furniture while we sat tormenting ourselves about what to do.

We definitely had to get out of the house because the owners were returning. We would take a big loss if we tried to get a refund on the tickets, and we would not have enough money to book passage on another airline. Finally I said to my wife, "They've got to be kidding. To hell with it. We'll stick to our plans."

She was against the idea. She accused me of risking the lives of little, unsuspecting children, not to mention her own. The only way I could get her on the plane the following day was to spend all the money I had left on liquid encouragement. And I needed a considerable dose myself. The kids, of course, had no idea what was happening and carried on in their merry ways.

And to this day they are still carrying on, oblivious to the crude realities of life on and above this earth. "So what was the big deal—there was no bomb," said my daughter Velma when I told her the story, thinking it might discourage her about going to Florida.

"You never know about these things. Life is tough. You have to be careful and sensible," I said, "and you can't just go throwing your money away like you want to do."

Well, she went to Florida in any case. And she did run into trouble. Changing planes in Boston she was informed that the flight to Miami had been over-booked. "You see, I told you not to go," I snapped into the phone when she called from Boston. "Maybe this will teach you to listen to me for a change."

She broke into a hysterical laugh. Then she explained that she was continuing on the next flight to Miami two hours later. Meanwhile, she had been reimbursed $240 U.S. simply for the inconvenience. Since she had paid for her ticket in Canadian funds, it meant that she not only had a free trip but about $75 to boot. I was astounded.

"That's life, eh Dad?" she said, still laughing.

California

"Absolute madness'" I shouted at my 19-year-old daughter Velma and her friend Bridget Blue when they came up with the ridiculous idea of travelling to California and back by themselves in a broken-down 1972 Ford Capri. The mechanic at the local garage was even more explicit. "I wouldn't guarantee 200 miles," he said.

Two days later, after rounding up a tent, sleeping bags, a camp stove and various other paraphernalia, including a few tins of Quebec maple syrup, they left. My wife and I were utterly dismayed, but we did manage to extract a promise that they would telephone us and Bridget's parents regularly.

The first leg of the journey went surprisingly well. The girls made it all the way to my wife's parents' place in Detroit, where they remained for a few days, shopping and visiting relatives and being fussed over by Grandma. When my daughter called, I reasoned with her that they had now made a good trip and should return home. I felt confident that if they didn't listen to me, then tough old Kentucky hillbilly Grandma would talk some sense into them.

That's when I discovered that the so-called generation gap can get you coming and going. My mother-in-law, 75 years old, not only didn't talk any sense into them, she was ready to squeeze into the back seat and head for California too.

Having lectured for two summers in Colorado Springs, I had good friends there, and I felt that the girls would be safe if somehow they got that far. But how on earth would they cross the vast prairies to that spectacular setting where towering mountains, like awakening dinosaurs, rise abruptly from the flatlands? But the reports came in—Indiana, Illinois, Missouri, Kansas—and there they were in Colorado Springs. I gave them telephone numbers of people at Colorado College, suggesting that they might get a cheap room in one of the residences for a night or two, whereupon they should plan to head back home, because they had already pushed their luck.

Little did I know how much luck they had to push. The first person they phoned, Dr. Joe Gordon, invited them for dinner and told them that he would be grateful if they moved into a house which he was tired of watching over for a colleague away on a trip. Velma and Bridget thus spent about a week in the beautiful resort town of Colorado Springs, playing tennis, horseback riding, visiting Pike's Peak, being entertained, having the time of their lives. Then off they went again, across Utah and Nevada and finally into California.

"Now that you've proved your point, come right back home," I pleaded on the telephone, visions of cultist kidnappers and mass murderers hammering in my head. Incredibly, however, they ended up with yet another free accommodation in San Francisco. A Mrs. Potter, the mother of a friend of Bridget's father, happened to be visiting Quebec. "Tell them to phone my son Glen and he'll give them the keys to my house," she said. Glen also took them to Fisherman's Wharf, for a ride on the famous cable car, and out for dinner.

By then I had given up on trying to talk sense. When the girls told me that they were heading south to Los Angeles, I simply mentioned the name of an old friend, Donald MacLean, from the East End of Montreal like myself, who used to play five-string banjo in the Blue Sky Café, the Bal Tabarin and various other clubs in Montreal back in the late fifties. I knew that he lived somewhere in Irvine, California, and I knew that he had two sons.

The next report I got was from Donnie himself. Three thousand miles of telephone cable did not diminish the joy in his voice. He and his wife Barbara were delighted to have visitors from back home in Quebec. At that moment, my daughter and Bridget were out seeing the sights with his older son, Scott, who was 22 years old and six foot one.

For several days the girls were wined and dined and regally entertained by all the MacLeans. They saw Venus Beach, which apparently has a section of pavement where people do acrobatic dances on roller skates. They dropped in at a Punk Rock place and saw women with hair cut down to bristles and safety pins in their ears, wearing leather mini-skirts. They also saw the lush California countryside.

On the way home, the girls visited the Grand Canyon, and after pit stops in Colorado and Michigan, they drove up the dirt road in front of our home, having chalked up some 11,000 miles. What can a father say?

Clearly the trip was a marvellous, enriching, vital experience. But given the brutal reality of automobile accidents, robberies, rapes and murders on highways, I could not recommend such a trip to two young women, even if they were driving a tank rather than a dilapidated little car.

On the other hand, there is something deeply reassuring about the hospitality lavished on my daughter and her friend. For years we've had the house full of teenagers and migrants of various descriptions brought home by our five children, and on occasion my wife and I have lost patience. It won't happen again.

My grandmother had a saying about that—something about casting your bread upon the waters. And speaking of my grandmother, as I've mentioned before, she left Scotland on a tramp steamer with one son and seven daughters, pregnant with my mother, to follow her husband to Montreal. She would have been proud, I suspect, of her great-granddaughter.

A Woman and a Half

Twenty-one years ago I was sitting in the waiting room of the Sherbrooke Hospital maternity ward. Since my wife had already presented me with two baby girls over the previous two years and eight months, I was an experienced veteran, calm and composed, patiently re-reading ten-year-old copies of *Reader's Digest* while the other expectant father in the room was chomping up the filters of his cigarettes.

When the obstetrician appeared at the door of the waiting room, I got up leisurely, but his announcement knocked me right back into my seat, dumbfounded. "You have three girls," he said. "Congratulations."

Immediately I thought triplets. Added to the first two, that would make five girls, and all within three years. My mother had been the last of nine sisters, and counting my father's second family, I had one full sister and seven half-sisters myself. Now it was shatteringly clear that I was well on my way to repeating, perhaps even surpassing the girl-siring feats of my forebears.

The doctor, however, soon clarified his statement. What he had meant to say was that I now had a third daughter, making a total of three girls. The tiny baby was especially bouncy, with a radiant sparkle in her eyes. We named her Velma Claire.

She had been three weeks overdue on that spring morning 21 years ago, but she has been making up for lost time ever since. Another spring morning not quite three years later, while I was taking my first sip of coffee after getting the two older girls off to kindergarten and school, and my wife was busy with yet a fourth baby girl, the telephone rang. It was the woman who ran the store in the middle of our small town, about a mile from our house.

"Does your little blonde daughter go to school?" the woman asked incredulously.

"Of course not," I replied. "She's not three years old yet. She's upstairs asleep in her . . ." "She just walked past the window with a couple of books under her arm and a lunch bag," said the store lady.

I rushed to Velma's bedroom, and sure enough it was empty. Convinced that my wife and I would surely be charged with child neglect, I jumped into my car and intercepted my little daughter just as she was starting up the front steps of the school. And I still don't know how she was able to put on her Sunday dress, prepare a lunch and sneak out of the house without either my wife or me noticing.

But we couldn't help noticing her later exploits, some of which I have already described, such as when she and her friend Bridget drove a $200 remnant of a Ford Capri all the way to California and back. They stopped over in Detroit, site of 600 or so murders a year, where 75-year-old Grandma crawled under the car and repaired the muffler with a tin can. What hope is there that she'll ever listen to my good advice, I told myself at the time, when even my mother-in-law is egging her on.

Two weeks after returning from the West Coast, she totalled the car against a cement barrier at a toll booth on the Eastern Townships Autoroute, and I had to pay $50 to have it towed away as junk. Then she went back to college, and my life was mercifully uneventful for a little while, until just before Christmas, when she took a notion to blow all her earnings from part-time jobs on a trip to Florida.

"That's ridiculous," I said, explaining that when I was her age I had to save for a month before taking the streetcar to the Capitol Theater in downtown Montreal. Walking over the Jacques Cartier Bridge to St. Helen's Island was a major excursion in those days. The limits of the universe were Bout de l'Isle to the east, N.D.G. to the west, Rawdon to the north and Brome Lake to the south.

Velma obviously inherited her stubbornness from her American grandmother, who spent her childhood with mules on a farm in Kentucky, but I don't know where she got her incredible luck. As I've already described, she was bumped on the Boston-to-Miami lap of the flight to Florida and was refunded the entire fare in U.S. dollars for a two-hour delay.

Sandwiched in the middle of a family of five, I guess that Velma has had to push a little harder than the others for attention. Blessed with a fine physique, she has always excelled in sports, and even though she didn't get to start school as soon as she had planned, her academic accomplishments have never failed to make the old man bubble with pride.

As a matter of fact, thinking over the last 21 years, I begin to wonder if the obstetrician's startling announcement contained more truth than he or I realized at the time. Velma Claire may not be three girls, but she's certainly a woman and a half.

Sympathy for Uncle Jack

He's been gone for more than 25 years now, my Uncle Jack, who adopted me when I was a small boy, but in the last few weeks I've developed a profound sympathy for him. The explanation is my own son, Colin George, who came after four sisters and is now 16 years old.

One night, alone in a small sailboat, my son took the crazy notion to visit a girlfriend called Danielle, who lives at the opposite end of 11-mile long Lake Massawippi. I've explained to him many times that at the age of 16 I devoted myself to books and to improving my mind and had no time to waste on girls, but I don't seem to manage a convincing enough tone.

At about nine o'clock, the girl phoned to say that Colin had been delayed because the wind had died down. But then it had suddenly picked up again, so he was now on his way back up the lake. Well, the wind had picked up all right. Trees were bending first one way and then another as ominous black clouds blotted out the light of the moon. The waves were crashing against the dock when I went down to the shore and strained my eyes for the sight of a small boat in the expanse of darkness. After a couple of hours, it was clear that Colin was not going to make it home. I went back to the house, and needless to say, my wife and I spent a sleepless night. We tried to reassure one another. I reminded her that our son was a powerful swimmer and that his feet were about the size of the flippers used by scuba divers.

"But he's just a little boy," she moaned.

We didn't get news of our "little boy" until mid-morning, when a woman from one of the telephoneless cottages along the lakeshore dropped by to tell us that Colin had landed at her dock and spent the night. He was still asleep, but he would sail home as soon as he got up and had a bit of breakfast. Profoundly relieved, my wife and I felt duty-bound to caution the lady about breakfast. Like the humming-bird and the shrew and various other ravenous creatures of the sort, our son can consume more than his body weight in a normal day.

"Great fun," was his comment when he arrived home, followed immediately by "What's for lunch, Mom?"

The incidents are recorded by the white hairs in my beard. Such as the time when he was two years old and slipped out of the hotel in a town in Scotland. "Hello, hello, you must be Mr. McCallum," said the smiling constable when I arrived at the police station, where my son was happily perched on top of the desk with an all-day lollipop in one hand and an ice-cream cone in the other. Apparently when the policemen asked him his name, he kept repeating "Me Colin."

While we were living in the Florida Keys, I ended up frantically calling the U.S. Coast Guard. He and his friend Miles DeNora had taken the boat out for "a few minutes" to see the sunset. Two hours later, scanning the shark-infested, shoal-filled ocean with binoculars, I could see no sign of the boat. I drove my car down to the shore and kept blinking the head-lights in case the boys were having trouble locating the dock. All the neighbours came out with flash-lights. We watched sombrely as the big Coast Guard launch, floodlights beaming back and forth across the water, moved among a cluster of tiny mangrove islets three or four miles offshore.

By about 10:30 p.m. we were all sitting around the kitchen table in despair, each of us afraid to speak, when Colin and Miles casually walked in the front door.

"Is there anything to eat, Mom?" my son asked.

It was one of those moments in life when a person is torn between two equally intense and totally opposite urges—I didn't know whether to strangle him or hug him. The boys had not been on the ocean at all. They had simply gone along the shore a few hundred yards to a neighbouring resort complex and had been playing tennis or basketball or something. They couldn't fathom what all the fuss was about. And it has dawned on me recently as I think back, that when I was 16 years old, occasionally there were happenings I couldn't fathom. Such as why my Uncle Jack used to get upset over nothing.

Poor old Uncle Jack was totally distraught when I defied his wishes, took all the money I had saved from newspaper routes and part-time jobs, and bought a used, 500 cc, Ariel Red Hunter twin-cylinder motorcycle. He warned me over and over again that I would smash myself up, and he was absolutely right. But for several months before the accident I raced across the country in the fast lanes, a variety of young things on the back seat clinging to me for dear life, and it certainly was "great fun" while it lasted.

Of course, I never breathe a word about that to my son, and I can appreciate now what my poor uncle had to go through. Come to think of it, though, Uncle Jack used to tell me solemnly that when he was 16 he was attending a strict, no-nonsense school in Scotland and had no time for anything except homework . . .

Zachariah and the Floods

My month-old grandson, who at the moment seems altogether too tiny for his resounding name of Zachariah, has at least two things going for him. On my son-in-law's side of the family he is a direct descendant of the Miles Standish who came to Plymouth Rock in 1620 on the Mayflower. The old Puritan would be startled, perhaps, to see his progeny not in the mighty nation founded by the Pilgrim Fathers but in a remote, rural area of French Quebec, but he would certainly be pleased that the little fellow is named after an Old Testament monarch.

On my daughter's side of the family, there is nothing quite so distinctive, I'm afraid. From my Kentucky-born wife and me she does pass down to her son and our first grandson a fair measure of fertility and hardiness—the child has literally hundreds of great-grandparents, great-uncles and -aunts, cousins, second cousins and whatever. But mainly he has ethnic variety, including Highland Scots, Irish, Italian, Dutch, German, French and North American Indian.

But the other significant factor he has going for him is that he was born in the Year of the Great Floods. In fact, my daughter and her husband had brought him to visit at the family home the very night that the waters rose in the Eastern Townships of Quebec. We had a late, long and leisurely dinner, too involved with the baby and each other to pay much attention to the rain outside. Finally the young parents wrapped up the child, and the rest of us stood on the veranda and waved goodbye as they drove into the pitch-dark, soggy night.

The next morning I was awakened by my son, who goes to school 15 miles away in the city of Sherbrooke and has to take an early bus.

"Dad, the road has disappeared!" he shouted from the front door.

"Don't talk nonsense! Get your backside out of here or you'll miss your bus again," I shouted back, still half asleep. My son has been known to resort to some devious strategies to avoid going to school.

"Come down and see for yourself," he replied.

It was a devastating sight. Tons of gravel had washed away from under the road, causing large patches of asphalt to buckle and cave in. At the bottom of our sloping driveway, the lake had risen eight or nine feet, flooding most of the lakeside road. Boats, staircases, wharves and boathouses were floating away.

My son and I were soon joined by my wife and daughters, then we all rushed back into the house and turned on the radio to learn that downtown Sherbrooke was under fathoms of water. So were a number of smaller towns in the region. People were being rescued by boat from second-floor windows and rooftops. Trees, cars and trailers were being swept downstream by swollen rivers, and on one farm where two rivers converge, 150 prize Holsteins had been drowned. Apparently a dam had burst, and the water had risen to above the level of the top of the barn door before the cattle could be released. Although cattle are actually quite capable swimmers, no amount of effort could induce them to dive under the lintel of the door.

And then came the news item which struck us personally—the North River Bridge, on the road to my daughter's and her husband's house, had been totally destroyed . . . sometime last night.

We gathered around in panic as my wife telephoned. The line was busy. We tried frantically to remember the names of neighbours. But at the next try, the call went through, and to our profound collective relief we learned that the young couple and the baby had made it over the bridge just in time.

They were all safely home, where they intended to stay until the floods subsided and the work crews made the roads passable again. The baby, no doubt tired out from all the attention received earlier in the evening, had slept through the whole adventure.

Local newspapers reported that the year's flooding in the Sherbrooke area was the worst ever recorded, several inches higher than the famous flood of 1942. Miraculously, however, not a single person was injured. We all survived the Great Flood.

And little nine-pound Zachariah? Well, I don't doubt that there will be more floods and God knows what other obstacles down the road for him, but I feel confident that the pattern has been set. He will cross his bridges before the rising waters sweep them away.

Being Wrapped Around Little Fingers

When the last of our children was finally out of
diapers, my wife and I celebrated. The worst was
over, we told ourselves. Never again would we be
jolted awake in the morning after a late night by a
toddler desperately in need of a seat-cover change
crawling over our heads.

Five children in six years had strained all our
resources. Not that we weren't into planned parent-
hood, because even in those pre-pill days we planned
carefully and in considerable detail, putting our faith
in rhythm, rightness and restraint. We planned to have
one son, then a few years later, one daughter, so that
child-raising would be over and done with while we
were still young enough to enjoy the freedom. We
had even the name picked for our first baby. He was
to be called Robert.

But we were obliged to make a quick readjust-
ment when the baby was born, and we called her
Janet. We would save Robert for the other one, we
resolved, then when the occasion arrived, somehow
two or three years before we had intended, Katherine
was more appropriate a name.

I came close to fainting after the delivery of our
third unplanned child. As I've mentioned before, the
doctor told me I had three girls, and I thought that he
meant triplets instead of a third daughter. Once we
sorted that out, we named the new baby Velma, still
holding Robert in reserve.

After Winona was born, we gave up on Robert
and on our old system of birth control. Already there
were two more than had been planned. But all our

best intentions, reinforced by masses of information and a new 99-percent-sure device, did not prevent a fifth child. And when the fact eventually sank in that he was a boy, we took several days to settle on the name Colin.

He now wears size 12 shoes, at $50 a pair for the running type which last a whole two weeks or so, and is in CEGEP or junior college. Daughters Two, Three and Four are at university, and I now know that getting them out of diapers was not the end of troubles but the beginning.

Many years ago, with a view to teaching our children financial responsibility as well as keeping them off our backs, my wife and I worked out a precise system of indexed allowances. But then a tiny tot with a ribbon in her hair would unleash a radiant smile and ask me for an extra nickel or dime, and of course she would always get it. They had me wrapped around their little fingers, I'm afraid. They still have, only now it's not a nickel or a dime but $500 for living expenses in "rez," $685 for a semester meal ticket, $100 for winter boots, $200 for skis.

Since we live in a somewhat isolated village, transportation is a headache. To avoid spending a good part of my life providing taxi service, or else becoming a nervous wreck as I sit waiting for one of my children to come home with the car, I invested a tidy sum in three second-hand—used is the more accurate term, I guess, because all of them had been through at least a dozen hands and probably a few feet besides—jalopies.

The first is now rusting in a back yard, having been ordered off the road by the police. The second came to an inglorious end when my daughter Velma tested it against a cement pier at an Autoroute toll station. And the third was wrecked by a horse. An old rickety Vega largely composed of fibreglass body-filler and mesh, my daughter Janet was driving it along a country road when she had to stop for a troop of equestrians. Then one of the horses simply backed up and planted his rump on the side of the car, caving in the roof and the door and pushing it into a ditch.

Meanwhile my son, growing at an alarming rate and into body-building now, can never seem to get enough to eat. My wife has to float a loan to go grocery shopping. He has informed me that my precious stereo system, which has brought me exquisite pleasure for 20 years, is "the pits" and must be replaced immediately so that he will not be the laughing-stock of his friends. My highly clothes-conscious daughters do earn a lot of their own money now, but from my wife's hillbilly horse-trader side of the family they have inherited a special cunning, and they operate a system of borrowing and lending and finagling of finances which inevitably leaves me without enough money in my pocket to buy a newspaper.

And as I write this, the latest development is right under my chin. My oldest daughter, now married, has come to visit with her baby boy, Zachariah, and she has plunked him on my lap so that he can "help old Granddad work."

My God, I can't keep myself from thinking as I try to type with one hand, it's about to start all over again! What happened to all our careful plans? But I must admit that the tiny fellow has a disarming smile. He really is a handsome baby. Certainly he has a strong grip as he wraps my beard around his little fingers.

The miseries of winter descended on my little village in the Eastern Townships of Quebec with diabolical vengeance during the holiday season. All day long heavy snow competed with freezing rain, both of them whipped into frenzies by the high winds. Anticipating the usual breakdown in hydro service, I placed two big maple logs in the fireplace.

With the idea of whetting my appetite by a bit of exercise, I then put on my boots and parka, pulled up the fur collar, and went out to clear the walk and driveway. As I shovelled I could hear the whining of a motor and the grinding of tires—a car was stuck somewhere in town. Needless to say, the roads were a mess. But what did it matter? For the first time in many months my wife and I had our entire brood gathered around us, plus our son-in-law and handsome grandson. My wife had prepared an excellent holiday meal, I had remembered to chill the wine, and now it was time to sit around the roaring fire and enjoy refreshing aperitifs before dinner.

"Thank God nobody has to go anywhere on a night like this," I said as I hung up my parka and headed for the kitchen to mix the drinks.

"Didn't I tell you, Dad?" announced my daughter Velma. "My friend Rob at MacDonald College is taking the five o'clock bus from Montreal to Magog."

Generally North Hatley is a lovely little town, a clutch of old New-England-style houses nestled in the foothills of the Appalachians on the shore of Lake Massawippi. But it happens to be at the isolated point of a triangle with Magog and Sherbrooke, where the two closest bus terminuses are located, and visitors without cars simply have to be picked up at one terminus or the other. The express bus from Montreal stops at Magog then continues to Sherbrooke.

"Ah...ll right!" drawled my daughter Kate—she'd been studying drama in New York and had picked up a number of stylish drawls—"my friend Georgina and a friend of hers called Balfour, who just blew in from Jamaica, are taking the same bus to Sherbrooke."

"Good Lord! Get on that phone quick!" I yelled at Velma. "Tell Rob to stay on the bus until Sherbrooke. At least get them all to the same bus station."

"I'm hungry," moaned my son, Colin. But no one paid any attention, because in his case the condition was chronic. My son-in-law, Greg, nobly volunteered to do the driving. Since the blowing snow was now causing near-zero visibility and the back roads were a sheet of ice lubricated by a layer of greasy mush, he left early. I abandoned the aperitifs, put on my boots and parka, and went out to shovel the walk and driveway again.

At about 7:30 p.m. Greg phoned from the terminus to say that only Rob had arrived. It was no surprise. A few minutes earlier Georgina had called, explaining that she had missed the bus and was taking a later one. "Hang in there," I told my son-in-law—I'd picked up a few new expressions myself—"No use coming all the way home then having to go right back." Then I put on my boots and parka to go out and shovel the driveway once more, inviting my son to help.

"I'm too weak from hunger to shovel snow," he replied.

"I was just thinking," said my daughter Janet, "this is the night that Michèle said she might come down. I told her to get off the bus at Magog, give us a call and we would pick her up."

That was when I took the phone off the hook. Then I thought about the fact that the Magog Terminus was actually just a small restaurant, and it would be closed by now. Could I leave a lone young woman huddled in a doorway all night long in a howling blizzard during the holiday season, while the rest of us were sitting down to a late but hearty dinner? I put the phone back on the hook . . . slowly. But it didn't ring again that night. A little before 11 o'clock Greg arrived with all four guests. "The roads are the pits," he said, "but the driveway sure is in great shape. Must be protected by those big pines."

"Let's eat," said my son.

Well, we finally did have dinner, then we retired to the living room with coffee and cognac and some kind of eggnog concoction which the kids had mixed up. I noticed that the young man from Jamaica, on his first trip to Canada and probably still in a state of shock, was staring out the window. I moved over beside him and my youngest daughter, Winona. The wind had died down. In the moonlight the landscape looked as if it had been sprinkled with tiny twinkling stars, and for a brief moment I relived a long-forgotten thrill of my childhood in the East End of Montreal, when I used to wake up on the morning of the first winter snow to see the dull greys and browns of balconies, staircases and pavement magically transformed into a pristine fairyland.

"Man, that's beautiful," said the Jamaican visitor.

I glanced around the room then out the window again. "Yes," I replied, "We Canadians love our winters." And at that moment, I was telling him no lie.

Bingo

I protested vigorously when the prize was handed to a fat, red-haired woman instead of to me even though I had clearly been the first to yell "Bingo." It happened at one of those small, travelling circuses called tombolas, and I was about 12 years old at the time.

"Get lost, kid," snarled the announcer, twitching his right leg and pushing me away.

That's how it has always been for me with games of chance and contests of various kinds. I thought that I had finally broken the jinx a few years ago when I sent in boxtops from a cereal and received a registered letter informing me that I had won a pool table. Excitement in the family rose to near frenzy after an actual phone call from the company wanting to know if I would sign a release to allow photographs to be taken when the table was delivered.

I replied that I would be delighted, beginning to wonder if the transport van would be able to make it up the dirt road to our home. My wife and daughters rearranged the furniture in the basement playroom, and my son speculated that we would have to tear out and rebuild the stair-case to allow elbow room for fancy shots. Certainly we would have to remove one of the basement windows, probably also the frame, to get the table into the house.

After two weeks of planning and mounting anticipation, the prize pool table arrived—not by delivery van, but at the damned post office! The package actually fit into our postal box. I don't recall the exact dimensions, but the balls were the standard little glass marbles used by children, and the cues were about the size of Chinese chopsticks.

Horse racing I tried once, during a summer when I and a friend were selling air conditioners and had just received our first commission. We went to Blue Bonnets and started off with two modest wins. Naturally our appetites were whetted. In fact, I promptly came to the conclusion that I had a hitherto unsuspected genius for judging race horses. I eyed the animals getting ready for the next race. One was a good six inches taller than the others, and it was so energetic that the jockey could hardly keep it under control. "That's our baby," I whispered to my partner, and we rushed over to the betting window with our entire commission plus the money we had won. "We'll never have to sell another wretched air conditioner in our lives," I assured my beaming friend.

And that might well have been the case, if only the huge beast had been the least bit co-operative. But to our utter dismay, it refused to run at all, simply standing there at the gate ignoring the jockey, tossing its head disdainfully and tossing away our fortunes at the same time.

Occasionally my brother-in-law, Keith Wilkins, talks me into a game of poker, and inevitably he ends up with all the cash I have in my pockets. He has ruined my coin collection. Once he even got away with my Canadian Tire coupons and two free car-wash vouchers.

For weeks one summer I took part in a trick cross-word-puzzle contest run by a Sunday newspaper. The tricky part was that most clues left several possibilities— four-letter word ending in *ire*, for example, with the clue "What managers do to coaches." The answer could be *fire, hire, tire* or *wire*, possibly even *mire* or *sire*. When the accumulated prize rose to enough money to get my car repaired and painted, I started sending in three or four variations in the hope that one would have the right combination of guesses. By the time the pot was sufficient for me to trade in the old car for a new one, I was buying a dozen Sunday papers.

I came close, I must say—one letter off when a winner was finally declared. But as my brother-in-law always says, close is only good in horseshoe games and dancing. He has a number of clever sayings like that to lighten the occasion as he is taking my hard-earned money.

I am, to be sure, only one of millions of losers in the games of chance which appear to be proliferating lately. I'm amazed that in these times of high unemployment, rampant inflation and general economic disaster, the Quebec lottery alone took in a reported $600 million or so last year. People surely must have better things to do with their dwindling finances.

Come to think of it, though, my car, as usual, is falling apart. Now that three of my daughters are off for the summer and have learned how easy it is to make collect calls, mainly to find out who has called them, the telephone bill is out of sight. The electricity account, which seems to double every time a new generator starts up at James Bay, is two months in arrears. The insurance premiums are due next week, and the municipal taxes won't be far behind. I was also hoping that it might be possible to put a little aside for my wife and me to have a modest vacation next year to celebrate our 25th wedding anniversary.

Now if I could just get a fraction of that multi-million-dollar gros lot. After all, somebody has to win. And by now perhaps the odds are in my favour.

Four Times Twenty-One

In just a few days now, my life will reach a point which I have dreamt about for many years—the last of my four daughters will be 21 years old.

I started dreaming about it while I was working in Leeds, England, for a few months, when my four pretty little girls ranged in age from five to nine and were constantly hounding me for thrupences to buy dreadful British lollipops which they called "sherbie-lollies." At the time, however, a maniac who attacked young girls was on the loose in the general area, and my wife and I were terrified to let the kids out of the house.

"What a relief it'll be when they're all grown up," we used to say to each other, neither one of us able to imagine that such a phenomenon would ever actually come about.

I was especially worried over my youngest daughter, Winona Lee, a tiny roly-poly thing who was always defiantly tagging along behind her older sisters, while the latter, despite all my orders, pleas and desperate appeals to sibling loyalty, were doing their diabolical best to get rid of her.

But they didn't succeed in losing her often. As she grew older, she became more and more defiant, scheming and persistent. Before long she had gained a definite edge in the continuing competition. For years, it seems, my major function in life was attempting to settle disputes over girls' clothes. My daughters had systems of exchange and borrowing more complex and incomprehensible than the workings of international finance. So many "wears" of one

191

item, for instance, might equal ownership of another, depending on style and occasion.

Winona's wardrobe expanded steadily, while the other girls appeared in danger of being reduced to their socks and nightshirts. The bureau and closet of her room were stuffed with their favourite blouses, slacks and shorts, and the remainder was distributed over every inch of the floor.

Meanwhile, like a butterfly emerging from a cocoon, she was transformed from a roly-poly raven-haired imp into a tall, statuesque young woman with long legs and broad shoulders, who excels effortlessly in every sport she chooses to try. Once when she won the cross-lake swimming race on Lake Massawippi, she swam back across the lake again to tell us about it. On another occasion, when we were spending the winter in the Florida Keys, she brought home a young man from a mid-western American university. A well-built fellow bubbling with self-assurance, he explained to me that he was on the varsity swimming team. I remarked that my daughter was also quite a swimmer, and he responded by challenging her to a race along the canal in front of our house.

"Yes, sir, your daughter is quite a swimmer," he muttered sheepishly as he climbed out of the canal about five yards behind her. But I guess it didn't do her much good, because we never saw that guy again.

She attracts attention without trying. In the National Film Board feature on novelist Hugh MacLennan, Winona is the girl on the tennis court with him. The film people noticed her talking to Hugh and invited her to be in the film. When Hugh finally gave up playing tennis, a sport at which he excelled, he gave all his treasured racquets to her.

Now that I think about it, I've spent a lot of time around tennis courts, shopping malls and many other places waiting for Winona, who has only the vaguest notion of time and is constantly striking up instant rapport with total strangers, distinguished, dubious and in-between.

When I was teaching in Augsburg, Germany, she came over to visit, flying People Express to London, then taking the ferry and train to Paris. Her overnight train from Paris, the reborn "Orient Express," generally filled with all sorts of sinister characters, was scheduled to arrive at six in the morning, and I was anxiously waiting to meet it.

But it didn't arrive when it was supposed to. Straining my limited German, I eventually found out that the Paris train had been delayed by floods. I sat on a hard wooden bench or prowled around the dreary station for nearly four hours, imagining a variety of horrendous scenarios, before my smiling daughter hopped onto the platform.

She, of course, had had a marvellous time, meeting all kinds of interesting people, receiving invitations to visit exotic places, having new-found friends buy her refreshments. She couldn't understand why her father should have been the least bit concerned.

In any event, my dream is about to be realized. The last of my four daughters will soon be a certified adult. But somehow there isn't the sense of relief I and my wife had expected.

In fact, to be totally truthful, I'd much rather be still handing out thrupences for sherbie-lollies.

Thick Skins and Hard Heads

To be hard-headed, meaning shrewd and practical, increases a person's chances to succeed in this world, I have no doubt, but I've discovered over the years that to be thick-skinned is also important—it decreases your miseries and thus quite probably prolongs your life.

Some people I know are constantly being upset by something or other—the expression on a store clerk's face, the blue slip from Bell Telephone about an overdue payment, a perfectly innocent observation that they're looking well now that they've put on a little weight.

Circumstances have thickened my skin. My mop of hair has never yielded to anything except glue, I have a limp from a long-ago motorcycle accident, I smoke a pipe and all the cigars I can get hold of, my dressing habits (I'm told by my kids) range from sloppy to slovenly, and I play the bagpipe. But I really don't care. In fact, I have on occasion turned it all to my advantage.

Once, for instance, when I was on holiday in the United States, I needed a knob for a stove. Knowing that Americans are notorious for throwing things away, I naturally took a stroll down a back alley on garbage-collection day. Spotting a likely pile of trash, I began poking around, excavating an assortment of knobs and all kinds of other valuable items. I became so captivated by the expedition that I didn't notice the lady of the house walk up behind me.

"What a pity," she agonized, shaking her elegantly coiffured hair. "Now if you had stayed in school and got yourself a little education, you wouldn't have to be doing that."

My immediate reaction was the inclination to point out to the lady that I had a BA., an MA and a PhD with distinction, signifying that there was nothing more I could possibly be taught, and that I was a member of a university senate as well as a department chairman. But I simply gave her a blank stare, which seems to come naturally to me and which countless years of education have made even blanker.

The lady then invited me into her house, served me coffee and tasty muffins, then even tried to slip me a few dollars when I assured her that I would definitely be looking into night courses. Which was the gospel truth, because the first thing I had to do once back home again was to organize the department's part-time courses and hire extra lecturers for the upcoming semester.

My wife, I'm afraid, could never have pulled that one off. I recall the time in mid-December when she was pregnant with our fifth, and I had to drive to the liquor commission to buy the refreshments for our annual department Christmas party.

As I was going out the door, the four children already born, ranging in age from two to six, all started screaming to go with me. Then, on the spur of the moment, my wife decided to come along for the ride too. It was a mild day and the car was only a few feet from the door, so the kids all piled in without bothering about their snowsuits and boots. My wife grabbed a shawl but kept on her comfortable bedroom slippers.

By the time we got to town, it was snowing quite heavily, but that didn't matter because presumably I was the only one who had to get out of the car. As it happened, however, I parked right in front of a department store, and my wife could not resist the temptation while I was standing in the long pre-Christmas line-up at the commission.

And that is how she came to be walking down an aisle in a skimpy shawl and wet slippers, dragging along four kiddies pitifully under-dressed for the winter, obviously pregnant again, shouting down tearful pleas for candies and everything else in sight because she didn't have her purse with her.

"Good Heavens! You poor soul!" exclaimed the kindly old lady who rushed over to her, reaching into her own purse for a pencil and paper. "Give me your name and address, dear, and I'll make sure that you're on the list for a Christmas basket."

I don't know what was my wife's indignant reply, but we certainly never got a basket. And I imagine that the kindly old lady's worst suspicions were confirmed when she saw my wife and the children get into the car at the same time as I arrived with a bag full of booze.

My wife, Jean, is obviously too hard-headed for her own good, a flaw in her upbringing no doubt. Now if she were as thick-skinned as I am, she wouldn't have to be hard-headed.

Or is it the other way around perhaps?

Travelling Lightly

Flying with Willie

The People's Airline, as Canadians sometimes used to refer to Air Canada, transported me efficiently enough from a conference in Cleveland, Ohio, to Toronto, where I was scheduled to connect with Flight 141 to Calgary, Alberta. We arrived at Toronto's international airport a little after six in the evening, allowing an hour or so to relax, pick up a newspaper, and browse around the shops before boarding the huge Lockheed 1011 for the West.

Now in this age of numbers rather than names and computer printouts to respond to cries from the soul, the Lockheed 1011—capacity 20F/269Y, range 3,650 miles, cruising speed 570 mph, two aisles and nine seats across, dull movies and two-dollar earphones— is the very epitome of technological advance and depersonalization.

But in a flying machine, especially one so enormous that by all rules of gravity and logic it should not be able to fly, that's not too bad. The thing takes off and lands by computer, I'm told, so at least I don't have to worry about whether the air crew's prolonged absences from home are giving them problems with their wives or husbands.

I was surprised to find nobody milling around the Air Canada counter when I strolled over to confirm my connecting flight. After all, the L 1011 holds 289 passengers. Where were they?

"There will be a slight delay on Flight 141," the Air Canada lady informed me.

"How slight?" I inquired.

"We have no definite information at the moment, sir."

"What's the problem?"

"We're having trouble with the equipment."

The equipment?

"You don't mean the airplane, do you?"

"Yes sir. The equipment is out of order."

"I see." My darkening countenance must have persuaded her to elaborate.

"We are now waiting for another aircraft to arrive."

"To arrive from where?"

"Vancouver."

"Vancouver, British Columbia?"

"We expect to be boarding about 10 p.m., sir."

That estimate, of course, proved to be optimistic, and by the time the replacement equipment was airborne, I was in a nasty mood, as were the other 288 passengers.

There wasn't a single empty seat. I began to wonder.

"The wife's been waiting at the Calgary Airport for four hours," growled the man next to me. "I couldn't get through to her."

Then the lights went out.

They flickered back on again just in time for us to see a steward and two stewardesses rushing with a tank of oxygen for an elderly woman who had apparently passed out three rows back. Even that was not enough to divert attention from the turbulence. Unusual for an L 1011, I thought, as the giant plane shuddered and shook, and articles rattled about in the storage compartments.

The expression "metal fatigue" kept popping unsolicited into my mind. It dawned or me that I had reached a point of exhaustion and exasperation, closing in on total despair. With more than three long flying hours still to go. I think that tears were forming in my eyes when the voice came over the loudspeaker: "This is Captain Morrison speaking . . ."

Could it be? I wondered. A quarter of a century, but still there was something about that voice.

You see, I used to go out with a Morrison girl who lived in a tiny Laurentian village north of Montreal. Her older brother, Willie, was the one who drove the gang of us to barn dances on Saturday nights.

Everybody knew everybody else in those days. The fiddler, Jimmy, was from a farm along the road. Between sets we all stepped out into the cool, pine-scented air, and someone would hand out cold beers from a cooler in a car trunk.

Willie was a great driver, always calm and controlled. He could manoeuvre the old Ford along the twisting gravel roads through storms and fog, while the rest of us cavorted and courted beside him and in the back seat. Although he could drive as well with one hand as most people with two, occasionally one of us would come up for air and shout, "Hey, Willie, both hands on the wheel!"

But we always knew that he would get us wherever it was we wanted to go. When he talked at all, Willie used to say that he had a notion to become an airline pilot.

A stewardess finally arrived alongside my seat with her little booze wagon.

"Could you tell me the captain's full name?" I asked.

"Captain William Morrison."

I lowered my seat to the reclining position and closed my eyes. The world shrank to comfortable dimensions. I was no longer 17G in an L 1011 on 141—I was snuggling up to a lusty, soft-eyed country girl in the back seat of an old Ford. She was whispering my name as she nibbled on my ear.

No need to worry. Willie knows every blind curve, pothole, drop-off and washout on every dirt road within fifty miles.

The girl put her hand on my shoulder lovingly, and I opened my eyes. "Hey Willie, both hands on the wheel!" I said.

"I beg your pardon, sir," answered the stewardess. She had that no-nonsense, we-are-the- goddesses-of-the-sky look. "Would you mind placing your seat in the upright position in preparation for landing."

"Not at all," I replied. "Marvellous flight."

And under my breath I whispered, "Nice and easy, eh Willie. And watch out for the potholes."

An Innocent Abroad

Sons and daughters often provide reflections of their parents, sometimes much more revealing reflections than does the mirror on the wall. Like myself many years ago, my 17-year-old son did Europe this summer, or perhaps it was the other way around.

I had accepted an invitation to lecture for three months at the University of Augsburg, a few miles from Munich in Bavaria, and the occasion seemed ideal. Colin had been working at part-time jobs to earn extra money. After school closing he would take the cheap People Express flight from Newark to London, visit friends in the British capital, then cross the Channel to Calais and Paris, where he had another friend. A couple of days in France, then he would take the new Orient Express to the ancient city of Augsburg, and with my apartment as a centre of operations, he would use his Eurorail Pass, which allows unlimited train travel throughout Europe, to visit as many as possible of the famous places on the Continent.

Naturally I worried about my son embarking upon his first major excursion away from home. Still, I tried to assure myself, he's now bigger than I am. I thought back to what I was doing at the age of 17, but that only made me worry more, so I concentrated on detailed advice and instructions.

I dug up maps of the subway systems of London and Paris, pointed out the various railway stations, told him about the exchange rates for pounds, francs and Deutsche marks, then I cautioned him above all not to lose his brand-new passport and travellers' cheques, explaining that in Europe the thieves could steal the milk and sugar out of your coffee and that Canadian passports were in high demand.

"What do you think I am, some kind of dummy?" he snapped back. "I can take care of myself. No way I'm going to lose anything."

He telephoned when he arrived in London, and I breathed my first sigh of relief. He had crossed the Atlantic safely and was enjoying himself immensely in the British capital. In two or three days he would pass through Paris on his way to Germany, and soon I would be showing him the old streets and Roman ruins of Augsburg, founded in 15 BC and named for the Emperor Augustus.

Six days later, no Colin. I called his friend in London only to find out that he had left three days earlier. After one more day of anxious waiting, I made a series of transatlantic calls to discover the name and number of his friend in Paris. When I phoned, Colin answered.

"What the hell's going on?" I shouted into the phone.

"You won't believe this," were his first words.

"Won't believe what?" I said, but I knew damned well what was coming.

"I lost my passport and my travellers' cheques."

He had been to the Canadian Embassy and filled out dozens of forms, but he could not seem to get a clear answer as to whether or when he would be issued a replacement passport. At one point he was told that the best idea was to fly back to Canada as soon as possible. He had also been to the French police, who had given him a paper stating that his passport was reported lost. At the bank handling the travellers' cheques he produced his lists, was given $100 and told to call back in a few days. By that time he had decided that the commercial announcing "Don't leave home without them," should more accurately be "Don't leave home at all."

While I was calling my son, a young German who had once lost his passport in Spain happened to be in my office. "Ask him if the paper from the French police has signatures and stamps on it," he said. It did, but it also specified that it could not be used as a travel document.

"Doesn't matter," said the German. "It's all in French. So long as it has signatures and stamps it'll get him across the border."

At my insistence, Colin boarded the next Orient Express, and when the gun-toting border official demanded his passport, he hesitantly handed over the police paper. The man puzzled over it a few moments, then took it away with him. After about ten minutes the official came back with the paper, and sure enough he smiled and said, "Sehr gut."

After eating steadily for two days in Augsburg to regain his strength, Colin came with me to the Canadian Consulate in Munich, where we managed to get him a replacement passport without difficulty. I had been to a reception with the Consul himself a few days before, and I judiciously tucked his card into my own passport before handing it over to the receptionist behind the bullet-proof glass.

It took three weeks and several phone calls before the rest of the travellers' cheques were reimbursed. Meanwhile Colin saw the museums, the monastery where Martin Luther defended his famous theses, the airfield where Rudolf Hess took off for Scotland and many other fascinating historical things. But his enthusiasm seemed less than perfect. He kept muttering about beaches and action. Finally he headed off to Italy and the French Riviera to make use of the Eurorail Pass during his last week in Europe.

When he called from Paris it was to tell me that the beaches at Nice were topless and that on the express train back to Paris from the Côte d'Azur he had to share a sleeping compartment with four young Swedish girls. He also mentioned that he had missed the hovercraft and would not be on time for the plane home from London. He would therefore have to go on standby and needed more money. Could I figure out a way to get it to him? Well, I did, but not without more complications.

The way he tells it, though, his European trip went without a hitch and he had the time of his life, especially on those wicked Mediterranean beaches. When I look in the mirror on the wall, I see a few more grey hairs, but when I consider the more revealing reflection, with a twinge of nostalgia I know that he is quite right.

Friendly and Unfriendly Skies

Today I phoned to make plane reservations. In itself that is no big deal, but in my case it proves once again that I am about as strong willed as an autumn leaf in the north wind. No wonder I still smoke my pipe and eat peanuts.

Last February I had resolved never to fly again. I was living at the time in the Florida Keys, a string of tiny islands which dribble off the southern tip of the sunshine state and are linked by the bridges of the "overseas highway" from the mainland to Key West. I had accepted an invitation to give a speech in Virginia, and after a dip in the warm ocean, I packed my bag and headed off by car to Miami Airport.

I drove past the palm trees and flowering bougainvilleas, past the Caribbean Club where Humphrey Bogart made the movie *Key Largo*, then as I started along the narrow causeway through the Everglades swamp, I turned on the radio. Alligators lurk in the ditches on both sides of the road, and the radio helps me to think about something else, while I drive slowly with both hands on the wheel.

Generally it is comforting to listen to the weather broadcasts in the Florida Keys. Bogart was there during the hurricane season, true, but that was only because he was playing a gangster on the lam. Nowadays the weathermen warn people to leave if there is any chance of a hurricane, and the rest of the time they exult in reporting the blizzards and other miseries being endured by the unfortunates in the North.

I was, in fact, enjoying the report of a terrible blizzard, relishing every detail—roads closed, telephone poles blown down, trucks piled up—when suddenly it occurred to me that all this was happening in Virginia, the very place where I was supposed to be going.

I almost swerved into the ditch, which would have given the alligators a chance to resolve my problems, but then I assured myself that the flight would definitely be postponed until conditions were favourable. That thought, however, brought back bitter memories of an event a few months earlier. I had been invited to talk at a huge conference in Toronto, and the date coincided with a television show on which I had been asked to appear. All expenses paid, generous fees, hotel booked, dinner with my publishers arranged—it was a dream come true, almost.

I took an early bus from the town of Magog, a few miles from my home in the Eastern Townships of Quebec, then the airport limousine to Dorval. The first ominous sign was the crowd milling about the Air Canada counter. When I eventually pushed my way through, I learned that all flights to Toronto had been cancelled or postponed because of a severe snowstorm blowing in from Lake Ontario.

But I didn't despair. I knew something that I presumed all the other frustrated travellers did not know—the Rapido train was leaving Montreal in an hour. It would stop at Dorval and arrive in Toronto in the late afternoon, but still in time for me to fulfill my commitments and collect my money. I rushed out of the terminal building and grabbed a taxi to the train station in Dorval. An incredible sight it was.

While a loudspeaker repeated that there were no seats available on the train, the line-up of unbelievers already stretched out of the station, down the street, and half-way back to Montreal.

To top it all off, after a dreary bus ride back to Magog, I had to sit in the bus station for two hours waiting for my wife to pick me up. Presuming that I was in Toronto having a good time, she had decided to go shopping and spend the money she presumed I would earn.

In Miami International Airport, my first problem was to find the counter of the small airline which has flights to Roanoke, Virginia. "I imagine that it's postponed or cancelled," I said to the attendant after my half-hour search. I was speaking from bitter experience.

"No sir," she replied.

"But . . . I mean . . . Isn't there a great blizzard blowing everything away?"

"I have no information on that. You'd better hurry, sir. Your flight is boarding right now."

The storm must have passed, I told myself as I rushed to the plane. Before I could gather my thoughts, I was airborne, breathing deeply as the small aircraft battered its way through a heavy layer of clouds.

Then came the first announcement: "Ladies and gentlemen, we regret that because we are expecting a lot of turbulence there will be no bar service on this flight."

Before the sobering trip was over, I saw a stewardess sail three yards through the air and make a one-point landing at an altitude of 10,000 feet. While all the belted-in passengers were desperately clinging to the arm rests as the plane lurched and bucked like a rodeo bronco, the young woman had started to stroll down the aisle as if nothing unusual was happening. Two elderly ladies across the aisle had their eyes closed and were sitting so stiffly that I was afraid they had died of fright, but I didn't dare loosen my seat belt to investigate.

On most flights after a landing, the passengers are instructed to keep their seat belts fastened until the plane comes to a complete halt, but this time, after five minutes or so, the passengers, all of us stunned and frozen in our seats, heard, "It's okay. You can unfasten your seat belts now."

That was when I resolved never to fly again. But then I did have to get back home, and by departure time, the sun had re-established sovereignty over a clear, windless, friendly sky.

Actually, I quite enjoyed the return trip. I like to travel, meet new people, see new things, but I always love to come back home to my family. I suppose that's why I've reserved a plane ticket for another trip. I still yearn for adventure. And, of course, if you don't go, you can't come back.

Hotels

As described in one brochure, the excellent convention facility and hotel at Michigan State University, called the Kellogg Center, is a "substantial building." After checking the dates on the fire extinguishers and the doors to the staircases, then happily noting that a thick vine was growing up the outside wall right to the window of my second-storey room, I felt reasonably secure. Until, that is, I closed the door and caught sight of the words TORNADO WARNING in large letters on a sign attached to the back of the door.

There was a time when I used to think of hotels and motels as sanctuaries. Instead of being rudely jolted from slumber by my five kids battling over a pair of socks, a soft-voiced receptionist would say, "Your wake-up call, sir. Eight-thirty." The soap, my toothpaste, my razor, my own socks would all be exactly where I left them, and I wasn't expected to take out the garbage.

But in recent months I have had disconcerting experiences. Given a room on the 15th floor of the Inn of the Provinces in Ottawa, I came back from an all-day meeting and took a shower, decided on room service instead of going out to eat, enjoyed the meal thoroughly, and settled into bed to watch the late news on the huge, colour TV. A good bit of the news was about a horrendous fire in a Chicago high-rise hotel, illustrated by shots of helicopters and firemen trying to rescue panic-stricken victims on the upper floors.

When I got up to turn off the televison set, I noticed that a blizzard had risen. Snowflakes blasted against the glass door to the little balcony, and only the flickering hints of lights in the nearby buildings were visible. The weather outside made the bed even more inviting, and my eyes soon grew heavy.

Then the fire alarm rang.

I jumped up, pulled on my pants, socks and shoes and rushed out into the hallway to join everybody else on the 15th floor. The deafening clang of the alarm then stopped, and a clear, reassuring woman's voice came over the loudspeaker: "Please be calm. There is a small problem on the fourth floor which we expect to have under control in a few moments. Kindly remain in your rooms until further notice."

I saw others returning to their rooms, so I did likewise. Who would dream of disobeying such a mellow-voiced lady? Besides, I didn't want to look like a lily-livered coward. I sat on the edge of the bed waiting for further notice, listening to the wind howl, trying to dismiss mental images of towering infernos. But after about three minutes, I got up. "To hell with this," I said to myself.

I soon discovered that I am not as independent a thinker as I used to imagine. The staircase was jammed with hotel guests, some still in their pyjamas. The pace quickened noticeably as the descending horde passed the fourth floor. We all crowded into the lobby to watch firemen push through and head up the stairs.

Well, it turned out that someone had pulled the fire alarm as a joke, presumably inspired by the tragedy in Chicago. It worked so well that the joker must still be laughing. Apparently he did the same thing at three other downtown high-rise hotels. The capital of Canada is not as devoid of humour as we all generally believe.

Since that night I have always carefully checked the fire protection in hotels. But as I gazed at the TORNADO WARNING in the Kellogg Center, my heart sank. Weren't fires enough to worry about? I recalled the story of a man from California who put a quarter into one of those ridiculous, bed-vibrating machines in a motel in Quebec City. Unknown to him, the electrical circuits were being repaired at the time, and when the machine didn't work he simply went to sleep. Two hours later the vibrator circuit had been repaired and was turned on again, and it is said that people walking along La Grande Allée were somewhat startled to see a man running down the street stark naked shouting "Earthquake! Earthquake!"

Fortunately, I did not have to follow instructions on what to do in case of a tornado—stay inside substantial buildings, use corridors and smaller rooms away from windows, avoid flying debris. The weather remained pleasant, and there were no fires or earthquakes either.

But a thought did occur to me. Despite the marvels of modern technology, computers and satellites, buildings which scrape the sky and rockets which break its bounds to explore the mysteries of outer space, man's accomplishments are still not nearly substantial enough to cope with the basic forces of nature.

And despite the luxury of modern hotels, there are times when the traveller would definitely be better off in a nice, dry cave.

Clean and Green

"Brush your teeth and comb your hair. There's a full-grown bear about to take your picture at mile marker 92." That was the bizarre message I heard when my son stuck the antenna of his small CB radio out the window of the car. We were travelling across the state of Iowa on a four-lane highway with hardly a curve for 200 miles, past countless acres of seven-foot-high corn, at a speed admittedly a little higher than the 55 mph limit in the U.S.A., but cruising along with the flow of the traffic. In fact, a red Bronco had been the same distance behind my blue Wagoneer for the last 100 miles or so.

"Good Lord! Is that something about a bear at mile marker 92?" I asked my son, noticing that we had just passed 91. "Must have escaped from a zoo or a circus. This isn't bear country."

"I think that means a police car," my son replied. My foot immediately lifted from the gas pedal and the red Bronco flashed by, the driver gazing over inquiringly, no doubt thinking that I had suffered cardiac arrest or something. His look was somewhat less sympathetic a few moments later, when pulled over on the shoulder of the road after suffering actual arrest by a state trooper in a patrol car, he watched my Wagoneer pass innocently by. At that very moment I resolved to buy a proper CB radio for the car.

We soon learned the colourful CB jargon—"smokey" and "bear" for policemen, "spy in the sky" and "bear in the air" for aerial surveillance, "clean and green" for a highway without cops or other obstacles. "A full-grown bear about to take your picture" means a marked patrol car with radar.

213

But there is a lot more to having a CB in the car than being able to avoid speed traps. Truckers pass on information about accidents, traffic jams, road work and advantageous alternate routes. They talk about weather conditions, roadside restaurants, pretty waitresses, and sometimes they simply talk.

"Last time I was driving through the big cornfield," I heard one trucker tell another while we were crossing Iowa on the way back from Colorado, "damned if I didn't find God. At least I thought so at the time." He went on to describe how he saw a suitcase at the side of the road, pulled his truck over and went back to investigate. "Then just as I was about to pick it up, I heard a loud voice. 'Don't touch that suitcase!' commanded the voice. An' I froze in my tracks, 'cause I was sure it was the Lord talking to me. I shook like a leaf, I reckon, then I went down on my knees."

Apparently the trucker stayed on his knees until he heard a noise. When he turned, he saw "this hippie coming out of the corn pulling up his pants."

Travelling the highways of North America, especially with "ears on"—with the CB operating— certainly makes one aware that Canadians and Americans share a continental culture. In Quebec, incidentally, CB users have developed a corresponding jargon in French. "As-tu des oreilles?" means are you listening? A police car with radar is "un Kojak avec un kodak qui va prendre ton portrait." Another designation of the police, interestingly, is "les anglais."

But while we are all definitely part of the North American continental culture, there are still significant differences between Canada and the U.S.A., as I saw clearly illustrated when I went to watch the Pike's Peak or Bust Rodeo Parade in Colorado Springs. I had seen the parade twice before and greatly enjoyed the cowpersons on their fine horses, the bands, the floats, the chuckwagons and various other trappings of the Old West.

That year, however, the parade had an entirely new aspect, something quite divorced from the "Wild West." Then again, maybe not. Half-way through the parade came soldiers from the Fort Carson U.S. Army base near Colorado Springs. They were part of the 4,000 troops about to be flown to Central America for "military exercises." In jungle battle dress, even their helmets camouflaged, carrying automatic rifles which glistened ominously in the sunlight, eight abreast, looking lean and mean, they marched by— platoon after platoon.

At Colorado College, where I was teaching a summer course in creative writing, there was much criticism of the Government's involvement in Central America—the halls of academe were still haunted by the ghosts of Vietnam. Yet as the countless platoons of battle-ready troops marched up Nevada Avenue, the crowds of spectators cheered wildly.

And as a Canadian at that particular moment, I felt very much a foreigner, too smugly aware perhaps that the avenues of Canada, by sheer good fortune, are contrastingly "clean and green."

Airport

Airports can be fascinating places. I spent more than two hours the other evening at Dorval, watching an ever-changing cross-section of humanity mill through the Arrivals concourse and disperse into the city of Montreal. There were businessmen in three-piece suits with attaché cases, family groups, young people in everything from ragged jeans to stylish ensembles, couples of all sorts, a bevy of nuns in both black and white habits, two old ladies in long, dark dresses.

Most of the travellers walked briskly, presumably knowing exactly where they were going. The last I saw of the two old ladies, however, they were showing a wrinkled piece of paper with an address on it to a cab driver. They had probably come to visit a long-lost relative, I speculated, who was no doubt too sick to meet their plane.

I like to watch crowds and speculate on the dramas taking place in various lives. I would have quite enjoyed two hours at the airport had I not been waiting for my wife, Jean, to pick me up. With every passing minute I was becoming more convinced that she had either wrecked the car or forgotten all about me. And after 27 years of marriage, five kids and one grandson, the second possibility was perhaps even more disturbing than the thought of a smashed automobile.

I had been scheduled to arrive on the 6 p.m. Rapidair flight from a meeting in Toronto. But the meeting finished early, and I grabbed a taxi to the airport to go on standby for an earlier flight. On the way there we ran into a violent hailstorm, and

216

mumbling something about God punishing Ontario for changing the Tory Government the driver had to take shelter under an overpass on the highway. For a nervous flyer about to board an aircraft, the storm was not exactly reassuring, but it made me more anxious to get back to Quebec, where the weather is the least of our problems.

It's amazing how many people travel between Montreal and Toronto these days. The Rapidair lounge was packed. I got standby number 114, didn't make it on the 4 p.m. flight, but did get on the flight at 5 p.m. There had been, of course, no point in trying to phone my wife since I didn't know what flight I might be on. The backup caused by the hailstorm delayed take-off until 5:35, and when I arrived at Dorval an hour later, I immediately called the Epsteins' place, where my wife had stayed overnight. I was told that she had left quite some time earlier to meet my plane, so I rushed out to the sidewalk in front of the Arrivals area to watch for my familiar old blue Jeep Wagoneer.

By 8 p.m. I had not spotted it. I was afraid to leave the area because private cars are not allowed to park by the exit doors. By 8:30 I was tired and hungry. Thousands of people had passed before my eyes, and most of them were now enjoying dinner, or at least an aperitif. Even the two old ladies—the reason their relative had not been at the airport to meet them, quite likely, was that he or she had stayed home to prepare a superb dinner. Then I began to worry about my wife. Perhaps she was in hospital, unconscious, injured, disabled. My despair was cresting as I re-entered the terminal to phone the Epsteins again.

Just inside the door, I bumped into Jean.

"Where have you been?" she shouted at me.

"Where the hell have you been?" I shouted back. People began to stare.

I found out much later that she had arrived at the airport at 6 p.m. and parked the car. At the Air Canada counter she was told that the 6 p.m. flight from Toronto was delayed, but she wasn't told why, and she's even more nervous about planes than I am. So she waited in the lounge until the plane was announced, then she went to the exit ramp, only to discover that I was not on it.

"I've been right here worrying myself to death for two and a half hours," she yelled at me as we headed for the parking lot.

"And what do you think I've been doing for the last two damned hours?"

"You could have had me paged."

"Paged? I had no idea you were here. You could at least have checked the Arrivals area."

"You never listen to me, do you? Why on earth should I check the Arrivals when the plane you were supposed to be on was still in Toronto?"

"Because that's what anyone with any sense would have done."

"If I'd had any sense, I'd have never gotten married."

It takes about an hour to fly between Montreal and Toronto, but it took my wife and me a couple of days to get our feet on the ground again. The next time I have a meeting in Canada's metropolis, we'll be going together—probably by train. And I trust that by then God will have finished punishing Ontario.

The Spell of Lorelei

The Germans have a legend about a beautiful siren called Lorelei, who haunts a rock on the east bank of the Rhine, combing her hair with a golden comb and singing a song which entices travellers to destruction on the rocks and rapids. I have twice passed Lorelei's rock, and although I didn't see the lady herself, I'm sure that I got caught in a bit of her Teutonic spell.

The lecture tour was scheduled to take me to ten cities in Europe, highlighted by an address to the German Association of Canadian Studies at its annual congress in Grainau, a picture-postcard town at the foot of the towering Zugspitze in the Bavarian Alps. It began with a flight to London, where I delivered a kilo of spiced kosher corned beef, commonly known as "smoked meat," to an old friend and one-time Montrealer, whose husband then drove my wife and me to the train for Dover and the ferry which crosses the Channel to Ostende, Belgium.

We had chosen the ferry to see the sights, but all we saw for four long hours, apart from the initial misty glimpse of the famous white cliffs, were huge waves slapping against the windows. The shuddering of the vessel and the thunderous sounds as it rose up then crashed back into the sea at least smothered the moans of white-faced passengers.

At Ostende the information booth was closed for the night, but by dragging our bags from track to track we finally located the train for Augsburg, South Germany. Exhausted, we collapsed in our sleeping compartment and were awakened by the attendant just in time to disembark. We then took a taxi to our

219

hotel. When my wife exclaimed half-hysterically that the hotel was moving, I laughed and told her that we had simply been too long on buses, planes, boats, trains and cars. Then I walked across the room to the window.

"Good God! It *is* moving," I shouted. Looking down I could see giant excavating machines digging a pit in the adjacent lot. Every few minutes our hotel shook enough to make the chandelier wobble and the pictures flap against the wall.

Unnerved as I was, I managed to get my lecture ready, and after I had delivered it, our host at the university, Professor Jurgen Schäfer, launched a pattern of hospitality which would continue throughout the tour—he took my wife and me out for a lavish dinner, in this case the local Swabian cooking, accentuated by superb Bavarian beer.

The meal at the next university town, Erlangen, was equally delicious, followed by a spell-binding night of beer-tasting and enriching conversation with two young German professors, Dieter Meindl and Rudy Dietze. When we got back to our hotel, I noticed that I didn't have my small briefcase. I explained to Rudy in some alarm that all my notes, lectures, plane and train tickets, passport and travellers' cheques were in the briefcase.

"At least we have insurance for the tickets," said my wife. I thought for a moment. "The insurance papers are in the briefcase too," I groaned.

Rudy and I decided that the briefcase had to be in the restaurant. Carried away by our animated discussions, we had all forgotten about it. Since our train to Bonn the following day was at 10:00 a.m., Rudy would be able to go to the restaurant when it opened at 9:00, pick the case up and deliver it to the hotel in plenty of time. No problem at all.

When the hands of the hotel clock indicated 9:30 the next morning, and there was still no sign of Rudy, I went to the desk and asked the clerk to call the restaurant, only to learn that a young man had already been there and that no briefcase could be found. It was now 9:40. "I guess there's nothing for it," I said to my wife in despair. "We'll have to get in touch with the Canadian Embassy and explain that it was all a mistake to invite someone like me over here. We'll ask them just to send us home as quickly as possible so that I won't become more of an embarrassment to the country."

We both stared forlornly at the clock as the hand wiggled past the 45-minute mark. Exactly one minute later, Rudy Dietze burst through the hotel door. Clutched in his hand, my briefcase.

It had been caught in the door of his car on the passenger's side, and three-quarters of it had been hanging out as he drove around Erlangen frantically searching for it. His wife had spotted it when he returned home, not knowing what else to do.

The sun was shining brightly as the train for Bonn rolled along the storied shores of the Rhine and passed the rock of Lorelei. She wasn't there, of course. My wife commented that now that she's famous she goes to Paris to have her hair done probably. But I suspect that she spends most of her time casting spells in cafés where visitors are treated to sumptuous meals and evenings of conversation punctuated by countless steins of excellent German beer.

German Madness

King Ludwig II of Bavaria, before it became part of a united Germany called the Second Reich in the later half of the 19th century, was a big man. He was also eccentric and gay, apparently in both the old and the current sense of the word, and when he drowned under suspicious circumstances while swimming with a doctor friend, he had already become known as "Verrückt" Ludwig, or Ludwig the Mad.

Three of the castles he built in the foothills of the Bavarian Alps, one of which was the model for the Magic Kingdom in Disneyland, have become major tourist attractions. Lecturing for a semester in the ancient city of Augsburg, about 35 miles from Munich and close to the Alps, I had occasion to visit the "little castle" at Linderhof, and I found out for myself why the king was called Mad Ludwig.

Not that we don't have fancy places in my home town of North Hatley in the Eastern Townships of Quebec. Some of the summer chalets boast 10 bedrooms and 200 feet of lakeshore. The home built by the much-publicized "Arab of North Hatley," Saad Gabr, has been reported to contain furnishings worth 30 million dollars. But believe me, compared to any of Mad Ludwig's various accommodations, our showpieces are like outhouses.

"Now that is what we may call a king-sized bed," said the tour guide, hesitating for the expected chuckle from the hodge-podge of awestruck tourists. "Pity he had a hormone problem," remarked a witty Englishman near me. It was more like a football field. Forty women had worked five years to make the

222

tapestries hanging in the bedroom, and the gold and crystal chandelier was the size of a sugar maple growing upside down. Apparently Ludwig had a thing about privacy, or at least about not being disturbed by the servants. The table in his dining room is constructed on an apparatus which allows it to be raised and lowered through the floor to a kitchen below. Murals, ornate ceilings, paintings, statues, ornaments in gold and silver abound throughout the castle, highlighted by an enormous throne which looks as if it might at any time and quite appropriately ascend into the heavens above. An elaborate marble aqueduct brings cascades of spring water down the hill behind the mansion, cooling the vast bedchamber in summer. Mad Ludwig's tastes, to be sure, were not simple.

By contrast, the act which made another German famous in this general area of Bavaria, and around the world for that matter, is regarded as singularly simple-minded. The apartment assigned to guest lecturers at Augsburg University is located at the edge of the campus, not far from the renowned Messerschmitt aircraft plant and facing the very runway where Rudolf Hess took off to fly to Scotland in the naive assumption that he could stop the Second World War.

The runway is still there. But the grass and weeds now push up through cracks in the cement slabs. A flock of sheep graze around it, and one evening I saw a small marching band use it to practise. The only planes around are jet fighters from German and American bases which swoop by high in the sky and traumatize the sheep with thunderous sonic booms.

In the distance beyond the abandoned runway is a building which has legendary associations of its own.

It is the Landsberg Prison, where a little more than 60 years ago a detainee in one of the cells wrote a book called Mein Kampf (My Struggle), which would become the bible of the Nazi movement. The detainee's name was Schickelgruber, but he would soon become better known as Adolf Hitler.

They were all afflicted by madness, I suppose—King Ludwig, Rudolf Hess and Adolf Hitler. For many years after the war, Hess was the only prisoner in the huge Spandau Penitentiary, and the expense of millions of dollars a year to keep him there was another form of madness.

Madness, in fact, seems to have many varieties and vastly different consequences. The city of Augsburg, which celebrated its second millennium in 1985, was 50 per cent destroyed in the bombing raids of World War II. A few miles away, Dachau stands as a grim reminder of the horrendous legacy of one man's madness. Augsburg itself has come full circle—founded in 15 B.C. by Caesar's stepson as a military garrison for the Roman legions, it now has another military garrison, containing 20,000 American servicemen and their dependents. The madness continues.

Ludwig's castles are monuments to the fact that with enough money and power, ridiculous fantasies can be transformed into even more ridiculous realities. Compared to his compatriots Hitler and Hess, however, and to some of the leaders in the contemporary world, perhaps King Ludwig can be considered the least mad.

Caribbean Capers

Sunshine Canadians

Quebeckers, it has often been said, believe that if they have shovelled enough snow, frozen their toes and ears at least once every winter, voted on opposite sides in the provincial and federal elections, and lived their lives in a reasonably decent manner, then when they die they will go to Florida.

Now that I am spending a little time in the Florida Keys myself, I have discovered that a good number of my provincial compatriots are unwilling to wait until the roll is called down yonder—they are here already. And the Quebeckers have been joined by a fair number of Ontarians. The other night I had four fellow Canadians over for dinner, Bruce and his son Ken from Toronto, and Jean-Pierre (called simply J.P. by everyone here) and his girlfriend Nicole from a town near Quebec City. I had met and gotten to know the four of them together at a nearby marina where I often go to watch the deep-sea fishing boats come in.

We had a marvellous evening, eating, drinking, exchanging stories of distant blizzards and snow-bound highways, comparing suntans, telling jokes about various politicians. The conversation shifted back and forth between English and French, but with half of us being bilingual, communication was easy. When my guests had left, it occurred to me that there is a simple solution to the problem of Canadian unity—get everybody out of the country. Once they are in a foreign country, Canadians seem to get along with one another marvellously.

Although I must say that travelling to Florida is not always easy. With a view to hitting the road at the

226

crack of dawn, my wife and I and our five children packed the car the previous night. It was snowing lightly, a few symbolic flakes to celebrate the fact that we were about to escape winter and head for the land of perpetual sunshine. I had not, of course, bothered to put on my snow tires this year. What was the point?

The following day we stepped out the door to find that the celebration had deteriorated into an orgy—16 inches of snow and counting. My suggestion that we have a few more cups of coffee and wait until the ploughs cleared the roads was greeted with horror and utter scorn.

I braked and tried to swerve when I emerged from a cloud of blowing snow and saw a car half-way into the ditch, but I couldn't keep from skidding. Caught his back fender with a sickening crunch. Fortunately, I only dented the bumper of my own car, and by the time the police came and made a report, the snow-ploughs had already passed by twice.

I drove late to make up for lost time. Somewhere around Baltimore, all of us in a state of exhaustion, I took an exit marked Food and Lodging. I know now that some of these markers are placed expressly to break the monotony of super-highway driving and to add suspense to a long trip. We proceeded 15 miles along a narrow, potholed road searching for a hint of the promised lodging. A single light bulb illuminated the sign of the dilapidated old motel with a semi-circle of tiny cabins. "Yuk—sleazy!' my four daughters announced in unison, even though they rarely agreed on anything.

I could not help noticing that as one couple was leaving a unit, a car with another couple immediately pulled in. I got the distinct impression that this motel was not catering to the family trade. "Bet they don't even change the sheets," remarked my wife.

Fifteen long miles back to the interstate highway and on to the next exit with a lodging marker. This time it was a large, modern motel. I was too tired to do more than sign the travellers' cheques. As a matter of principle, despite a lingering Canadian chill in the air, we all packed our winter clothes into a kit bag before retiring.

Maryland, Virginia, the Carolinas and Georgia— by evening of the second night we had passed back through the seasons from winter into late summer. The grass was green. Even though it was a totally unnecessary service, I cheerfully tipped the motel bellboy after he grabbed a couple of bags, carried them a few feet to our units, and indicated the location of the ice machine. He responded with a radiant smile and vanished.

"You see how pleasant people are in warm climates," I pointed out to my family. "They get sunny dispositions."

"What did you tip 'im?" asked one of my daughters.

"A buck," I replied, "because I've no American change yet." Then I checked my cash. To my consternation I discovered that with the different denominations of American money all the same colour, I had inadvertently given the boy a $10 bill.

"No wonder he was smiling," said my daughter.

"All you have to do is look at the little numbers in the corners," added Jean, my American-born wife. I headed for the ice machine, only to discover that I didn't have a quarter to make it work.

Had it not been for a thick fog along the coast, we would have noticed the bright Florida sun right away.

By early afternoon, however, the fog lifted and finally there they were—palm trees, orange groves, huge red bougainvillea blossoms, cactus plants. We stopped at a roadside stand to treat ourselves to fresh fruit from this exotic, foreign land. The merchant glanced over at our Belle Province licence plates.

"Vous venez d'arriver, vous autes? You just get here?" he asked. He even looked like the man who runs the grocery store in our hometown.

The woman in the shop where we buy fish also makes us feel at home. She wears a typical Canadian parka when she goes into the large refrigerator room.

"I like you people," she says. She told us how a man from Sudbury arrived one day just when she was shivering from having to go into the cold room. He went back to his car right away.

"Here," he said, as he threw her the parka in an eloquent gesture which speaks for all of us happy, united sunshine Canadians.

Lobster Dreams

To become an adult, I used to believe when I was a small boy, meant that I would no longer have to wash behind my ears and that I would get to eat lobster.

An aunt of mine—I had eight of them—was once treated to a lobster dinner at a posh downtown restaurant for her birthday or anniversary or something, and the event was a subject of family conversation for years.

"Not bad," she would remark after a Sunday meal which I had thought especially delicious, "but you know, you really haven't eaten until you've tasted lobster. They give you a thing like a nutcracker to break open the shell and a tiny fork to get at the meat. Then you dip it in a bowl of garlic butter all melted." A glassy look would come into her eye.

"What does it taste like?" I always asked.

"Exquisite. Superb. Divine. There's no way to describe it. A taste all of its own," was the usual reply. And being too young then to think about girls, I put lobster into my fantasy file somewhere between swinging on a jungle vine alongside Tarzan and flying in an airplane.

Well, eventually I did get to eat lobster, three of them at the same time in fact. My family and I attended a gala dinner at a conference in Sackville, New Brunswick, and it turned out that all five of my children, to my utter amazement, did not want to eat their lobsters. "You should see how they cook 'em," said one of my daughters. "Dump 'em into boiling water while they're still wiggling."

"Never mind. Pass your plate over here then."

230

"But isn't it cruel, Dad? Doesn't it hurt 'em? How would you like . . ."

"Keep quiet now. Here's some money. Go buy yourselves hot dogs."

"They don't feel a thing," added my wife, muttering with her mouth full and reaching for the plate rejected by our second daughter, "I read all about it in a cookbook once."

Since then I have eaten lobster on a number of occasions, including the Caribbean spiny lobster or langouste, which I feasted upon curried and with slices of banana in a gourmet dish called *langouste à la Bombay.*

Once, while snorkelling off the Florida Keys, I and the oldest of my three nephews actually came upon what at today's prices was the next best thing to pirates' treasure—a lobster trap which had lost its marker float in a storm, making it fair game for any finder. Long antennas were sticking out through the slats like the quills of a porcupine. The wooden trap was literally packed with huge spiny lobsters.

Now this particular nephew, Bruce Wilkins, who later played for the Saskatchewan Roughriders and the Winnipeg Blue Bombers of the Canadian Football League, did not share my own children's qualms about crustaceans. And he had not built a 240-pound frame from eating lightly. He was even ready to tread water over the loaded trap, a half-mile out in shark-infested ocean, while I went back in the boat to get rope. Fortunately, however, I had a Styrofoam float in the bait box.

I called to my wife to get the big pot boiling as we headed back out with one of my daughters at the helm. Bruce and I jumped into the water, quickly tied the rope to the top of the old trap, then signalled to my daughter to head for home port "nice and easy."

I felt a surge of gleeful triumph as the trap started to rise, and even through the snorkel mask I could detect the look of excitement in my nephew's eye. We were about to pull it off. This was the biggest stroke of luck in the family for years.

In the next instant Bruce and I were diving to the ocean floor, frantically and futilely trying to catch lobsters fleeing in all directions. What we had not noticed was that the whole bottom of the trap had rotted away, and what we learned that day in the warm sea was that lobsters swim backwards and at incredible speeds.

Curiously enough, my daughters are now acquiring a taste for lobster dishes, especially when Dad is buying dinner. I'm leaning more and more towards spaghetti and meat balls myself. I suppose that is the way with most of the dreams of childhood. I would not want to swing on a jungle vine now, even alongside Bo Derek, for fear of putting my back out again, and I travel on planes only when there is no other choice.

If by some miracle I could talk to my boyhood self, I would tell myself frankly that being an adult is not all that it is cracked up to be. The lobster loses a lot of its flavour as time goes by. Soon enough nobody really gives a damn whether you do or not, so there's no joy in not having to wash behind your ears. And just when you think you've hit the jackpot, sometimes the bottom falls out.

Florida Fish Tails

Never having had the patience to fish, I have never been able to tell proper fish stories, even though my permanent residence is on the shores of Lake Massawippi in the Eastern Townships of Quebec and this winter, having been granted a sabbatical leave, I am living on the Florida Keys with the Atlantic Ocean a few feet from the front door.

The Florida Keys are known as a fisherman's paradise. Quite often in the late afternoon I wander over to a nearby marina to watch the deep-sea fishing boats come in, and I have learned that anyone seriously enough inclined can charter one of these boats, complete with skipper and crewman, for about $400 a day.

Once a boat has docked, the crewman, as a form of advertising I suppose, hangs the catch on spikes in a rack extending along the wharf. It is a pleasant diversion to meander past the boats in the warm sunshine, sipping a rum-runner perhaps, looking at the fish, and looking at the people looking at the fish. I have even gotten to know the names of the more common ones— snapper; kingfish; grouper, which seems to be the most popular for eating; and sailfish, which has a huge blue dorsal fin and is prized as a trophy to hang above the fireplace.

When my brother-in-law came down to visit a couple of weeks ago, I naturally took him over to the marina. With the casual air of a seasoned expert I dropped a few names and commented on numbers and sizes. "Fair-sized grouper . . . but I've seen 'em a lot bigger . . . must have been a bad day for snapper . . .

or else that skipper doesn't know the right spots . . . proper bait is important . . ."

My brother-in-law had done some fresh-water fishing and was impressed. "Wouldn't it be something else," he said, "if I could catch a fish like one of those? Get my picture taken to show the boys back home in the deep freeze."

"No problem," I said, "for four hundred bucks . . ."

"Are you nuts? Why blow a bundle like that? You know all about it. I'll just buy a line and some hooks, and you can show me what to do."

"Sure," I said, not having the slightest idea what to do. But as my old grandmother used to say: "It's an ill wind that blows nobody good." And the ill wind was in a cold front which plunged the temperatures in Florida to record lows. My brother-in-law, Keith Wilkins, a burly 230-pounder, had sun-burned his nose standing on the rocky shore trying to catch a fish. Now he was in danger of catching a chill. He had tried all the baits I suggested, but so far not so much as a nibble.

"I don't believe any fish are in there," he said finally.

"Don't be ridiculous," I replied. "The ocean's full of fish. Even an idiot knows that. You just have to know how to do it. Lines, baits, timing, expertise . . ."

"Right, let's go."

When he just about dragged me down to the shore and I gazed into the water, there it was— a giant grouper not six inches away from the rocky ledge, driven in from the open sea and apparently stunned by the cold.

"My God!" I shouted. "Look at that!" It was clearly the moment for expertise. I lay on my stomach and hung over the ledge, my brother-in-law holding my feet. I lunged for the fish, but it simply pushed into a hole in the rock, its tail still visible. We both had a go at grabbing the tail, but to no avail. He tried poking it with a stick, but the grouper wiggled deeper into the hole. Then I decided to tie a fishing line around the tail with a slip knot. My brother-in-law waded into the water and started to tug.

The fish backed out. I grasped for it and fell in. By then my wife had arrived with a net. All three of us were soon flailing around in the water. I still don't know exactly how we did it, but finally we got the big grouper on shore.

It was at least three feet long and weighed more than 20 pounds. We quickly untied the line from its tail, put a proper hook in its mouth and took a whole roll of photographs. Then we hung it on a lamp post in front of the house for a while.

"Beautiful grouper," commented one of the neighbours. "What kind of bait did you use?"

I pretended not to hear.

"The usual," said my brother-in-law, who is not above embroidering the truth at times.

He's back in Canada now. So if you happen to find yourself in a bar and a heavy-set, balding man named Keith is bragging about going to Florida and catching a giant grouper with his bare hands, don't swallow the story hook, line and sinker. Ask him about the expert fisherman who tied the line to its tail.

Hot and Cold Canadian Air

I now know why Americans arrive in Canada in the middle of July with skis on their roof racks and snow-shoes in the back seats of their cars. It's all the fault of the weather reports.

Here in Florida during the last few weeks the weather has been unseasonably cold. An elderly vagrant actually froze to death in Jacksonville at the northern extreme of the sunshine state, and although by the afternoon the temperatures, despite the cold spell, have generally risen to 70 or 75 degrees Fahrenheit, the other day I saw a woman in a fur coat. And me expecting bikinis.

In many ways, incidentally, travelling to Florida, or to any part of the U.S.A. for that matter, is like going back in time, to a more comfortable age when things made sense, when a foot was a foot and a two-by-four was three and three-quarters by one and three-quarters inches. They still sell gas by the gallon here, and measure distances by the mile, and the temperatures are given in real degrees.

The problem is that during a cold snap Canada gets all the blame. "Canadian Air Threatening Crops in South Florida . . .Vacations Ruined by Canadian Wind . . . Air Mass from Canada Making Life Miserable . . . Canadian Blast Causing Blackouts Across State . . ."—that's the sort of headline I've been reading daily in the Florida newspapers. No wonder Americans think of their northern neighbour as a barren wasteland of snow and ice. When it gets balmy here, the newspapers never announce "Mexican Air Making Everyone Sweat" or "Caribbean Heat

Wave Scorching the Earth." Instead it will be something like "Southerly Breezes Bring Warm Moist Weather."

There is really no excuse for this kind of misrepresentation and national prejudice. As everyone should realize, we Canadians do not manufacture our own climate. God knows, if we could, it would be quite different from what it is, and the multi-billion-dollar tourist industry in Florida wouldn't be worth a snowflake.

It should also be noted that when Americans refer to pure water, petroleum, natural gas and various other desirable substances found in Canada, more often than not they are called "continental resources." Cold air masses. on the other hand, are something to which Canadians are accorded exclusive rights.

"We don't mind you bringing your beer and cigarettes, your rye whisky and your vinegar to put on French fires. We don't even mind you bringing your husbands and kids," a shopkeeper told my wife the other day, "but I wish to hell that you'd leave your weather back home."

It's incredible really. Native Floridians actually believe that the weather they have been experiencing is not a true, natural phenomenon, but the result of some diabolical foreign-nation plot, like Hong Kong flu or German measles.

Still, despite little misunderstandings, life in the tropics has its thrills. Yesterday I found a live specimen of my own zodiac sign—a scorpion. It was under a jerry can which had been abandoned in the nearby mangrove bush. Since you never know when you might find something still useful or valuable, I have this compulsion to investigate trash. Especially in the United States, because Americans are marvellous litterers. They like everything to be brand new. Anyway, I picked up the jerry can to see if it had holes in the bottom.

The scorpion was shiny black. Its body was an inch and a half to two inches long, and the segmented tail, which it kept whipping into the air in an attempt to get me, was a good three and one half inches, tipped by an ominous stinger. I had heard that large black scorpions can sometimes kill a person, so I gently replaced the can, which was all rusted out in any case.

My wife, shuddering at the thought, had her own explanation of why scorpions grow so large: "How else could they handle those two-inch cockroaches?" Floridians, typically, call the roaches Palmetto bugs.

The incident got me thinking about a prominent Quebec politician's remark that Canada and Quebec were like "two scorpions in a bottle," and that in turn brought a flood of memories of various statements made by politicians back home.

But I immediately wiped them from my mind. It's enough having to contend with the cold Canadian air, I told myself.

In Search of Papa and Bogie

They weren't exactly idols, at least not in the sense
that teenagers today have idols, but when I was in my
teens I was quite intrigued by the macho/artistic
images of Humphrey Bogart and Ernest Hemingway.
They were, after all, a little more . . . well . . . manly
than Boy George or Michael Jackson. And now I find
myself in the Florida Keys about half-way between
Bogart's Key Largo and Hemingway's Key West.

The Caribbean Club, where the film *Key Largo*
was made, is still there, a modest little bar packed
with all sorts of Bogart memorabilia. It is back a
couple of hundred yards from the Overseas Highway,
which hops 138 miles from key to key (from the
Spanish *cayo*, meaning a coral islet) all the way from
the Florida mainland to Key West, only 90 miles from
Cuba. One of the connecting bridges, known as the
"Seven Mile Bridge," is actually about seven miles
long.

The ocean is the same, but just about everything
else seems to have changed since Bogart played in
the classic movie. Condominiums, fast-food outlets,
trailer camps, marinas, motels, resorts, real estate
offices, discount liquor stores, beauty parlours,
restaurants and flea markets line the highway. In
other words, the key has been "developed." Or rather
it is being developed, because the process continues
and presumably will go on until the last mangrove
marsh has been filled in and the last parcel of land is
graced by a mobile home.

To lure people to their condominiums, the devel-
opers have conceived ingenious schemes, including

239

time-sharing plans which permit those who can't afford to buy an apartment to purchase for only one-week or two-week periods each year. It reminds me of the custom of some African tribes whereby if a man can't come up with a dowry sufficient to marry a whole woman, he can negotiate for part of a wife, perhaps an arm or a finger. Immediate gifts of $25 cash, a $50 U.S. Savings Bond or 25 silver dollars are offered by various of the condominiums simply to tour the site and listen to the sales pitch for an hour or two.

A patient listener can pick up $100 or more in a day. In fact, a Quebec friend of mine did just that. What the salesman didn't know was that behind the pleasant smile and enthusiastic nods, albeit not always at appropriate times, lay almost a complete ignorance of the English language. But my friend could count U.S. dollars very well indeed.

If anything, Key West, the southernmost point in the continental United States, is even more commercialized than Key Largo, and Hemingway, to be sure, is one of the major enterprises. His erstwhile favourite bar, Sloppy Joe's (or at least the bar which now goes by that name), uses his photograph in its advertisements, sells innumerable souvenirs and once a year holds a major literary event—a Hemingway look-alike contest. For an admission fee one can visit the house where the famous American author lived and wrote in the 1930s, gaze at the typewriter which produced such works as *For Whom the Bell Tolls*, and at the 40 or so six-toed cats descended from the Hemingway pets.

When he was living there among the "Conchs," descendants of United Empire Loyalists who came to the Keys by way of the Bahamas and who survived modestly by fishing, boat-building, carpentry and wrecking (salvaging goods from boats smashed on the coral reefs), Hemingway once called Key West "the St. Tropez of the poor." Nowadays white Cadillacs and black Lincoln Continentals crowd the parking lots of posh resorts and hotels, while $100,000 yachts and cabin cruisers with teak and mahogany furnishings glide majestically in and out of berths in the vast marinas.

In striking contrast to this opulence, panhandlers, young people with backpacks, beachcombers and a variety of tanned vagabonds trudge along the shoulders of the Overseas Highway, plying their way among the empty beer and pop cans, broken bottles, paper, plastic bags and containers for suntan lotion.

Yet despite the extremes of shoddiness and ostentation floating on a sea of rampant commercialism, the essence of Bogart's and Hemingway's Florida Keys can still be found. Not in Key Largo and Key West, but rather in the many less populous islets spread over the ocean in between. While out in my little boat the other day, cruising among some uninhabited mangrove keys, I got caught in a sudden squall and ran out of gas at about the same time. As the boat rocked back and forth, from side to side and up and down simultaneously, I looked around for help, but there was no other boat in sight. I realized by the rapidly diminishing heights of the mangroves that I was being blown out to sea.

Wrestling with the spare fuel container, I managed to pour perhaps a third of the gas into the boat tank, and what kept running through my mind was the gangster's description of a hurricane in

Bogart's movie—"a big wind that puts the snatch on people."

Well, it was a big wind, and it made me realize that despite all the "development," nature was still in the driver's seat. Fortunately, it didn't put the snatch on me, and I felt proud of myself as I finally got the boat motor going again.

Then as suddenly as it had started, the wind died down, and within minutes the warm sea was calm. I turned off the motor and drifted for a while, gazing at the blue and turquoise shades of the water, basking in the sun under a now-cloudless sky, and enjoying a few moments of profound, primeval peace. And for those few moments I felt close to Papa Hemingway.

The Disgustingly Filthy Rich

Florida in the winter is the place to see not only the rich but the filthy rich and the disgustingly filthy rich. The other day I was invited to take time off work in the modest little house I am renting to ride on a modest fishing boat for the annual "Blessing of the Fleet" at Islamorada in the Florida Keys. The boat, called the *Swashbuckler*, belonged to Captain Scotty Kingsley, a seafarer we had gotten to know well and, I believe, the only woman fishing-boat skipper in the Keys.

The event is quite a contrast to what I would normally be doing mid-winter back home in Quebec. Fifty or so boats of every description gather offshore in the warm blue water of the Atlantic, then they form into a line and head along a channel towards one of the bridges of the Overseas Highway between the Florida mainland and Key West. The tropical sun glitters on the waves as the vessels file past the group of local clergymen standing on a spit of shore to dispense their collective blessings.

It is a marvellous way to spend a morning. We all enjoyed ourselves thoroughly—my wife and I, my 21-year-old daughter Winona, who is working down here as a waitress, and my two house guests, Roland Hill, a Mohawk steelworker and sometime chef from Brantford, Ontario, and Angus MacDowell, an engineer and fellow bagpiper from Montreal. Angus and I, of course, let the sound of the Great Highland Pipe drift over the sea to the cheers of fellow boaters and the people gathered on shore.

Then as we doubled around, we had a chance to gaze at all the other boats. There were several charter

243

fishing vessels like the one we were on, plus the cabin cruisers of the rich and the filthy rich. But at the end of the flotilla came a prize specimen of the disgustingly filthy rich—a private launch at least a 100 feet long, equipped with all sorts of elaborate electronic gear, teak furnishings in the state room, visible through the large portholes, and two lifeboats bigger than my own 20-year-old, 12-foot motor boat.

On the upper deck of the launch, standing with the owner, were a uniformed chef in one of those tall, mushroom hats, several mini-skirted maids who looked as if they had stepped out of a French movie, a butler serving champagne, and assorted other members of the crew. And to my surprise, the ordinary little guys watching all this from their campers, who had probably sold their souls to the finance companies for brief vacations in the sun, actually applauded what was surely a blatant exhibition of ostentation.

The explanation, it seems, is that the rich in the United States have more of a tendency, indeed more of an obligation to be disgustingly filthy than do the Canadian rich, who generally seclude themselves behind the hedges and granite walls of districts like Westmount or in their private clubs. It is almost as if they feel guilty about having more than the vast majority of the human race.

The American rich, on the other hand, are the embodiment of a national ideal. They feel no guilt whatsoever, and they love to flaunt their possessions both material and human. They are worshipped and protected by U.S. society. Thousands of them, I'm told, despite having the largest incomes in the land, pay no income tax at all. During the last month or so the newspapers have been describing the heart-rending plight of one Mollie Wilmot. An old cargo vessel called the *Mercedes* somehow beached on her oceanfront estate during a storm, doing considerable damage to her swimming pool.

What is heart-rending about it all is that salvage crews have not yet been able to refloat the *Mercedes*, and the poor lady's view has been marred for several days now. Mollie Wilmot, however, can at least take comfort in the fact that the State of Florida is not indifferent to her welfare. More than $250,000 of the taxpayers' money has been allocated to remove the eyesore.

The courts also seem to have special sympathy and concern for the problems of the rich and powerful. Just the other day I read about a man who was sent to prison for stealing three cans of sardines from a supermarket in Key Largo. Meanwhile John Zaccaro, husband of Geraldine Ferraro, the vice-presidential candidate a few elections ago, pleaded guilty of "scheming to defraud" in a huge financial deal and has been sentenced to a few hours of "community service."

But so far as the courts are concerned, I don't see a great deal of difference between the American and Canadian. That is probably because a major function of both justice systems is to protect what the "haves" have. The "have-nots," naturally, are ineligible for protection since they have nothing to protect.

The real difference between the rich in Canada and the United States is in attitude—their own and that towards them. "It's all in the way you think," a wealthy man explained to me. "Americans venerate the rich because that is what basically everyone wishes to be. And through the power of positive thinking, any one can be."

Well, I've been thinking positively, and I may have come up with a simple way to penetrate the realm of unlimited wealth. If it doesn't sink first, I'm going to take my little 12-foot motor boat to the next blessing for the fleet. I'll have my ironworker friend in a chef's uniform cooking hot dogs on a hibachi in the stern. My engineer friend Angus in full Highland dress will play the bagpipe while my daughter, in her waitress costume, serves sparkling cider to my wife and myself.

After we've been duly blessed, I'll invite the clergymen and their assistants on board for refreshments. I'll even invite the owner of the big cabin cruiser and his entire staff. And when the people on shore show their veneration, I'll invite them on board too.

Then I'll head the boat out to sea. We'll cruise the whole Caribbean—the Virgin Islands, Antigua, Guadaloupe, St. Lucia, Trinidad, Tobago—then we'll swing down the coast of South America and around the Cape to the South Seas. And when we've circumnavigated this world, I'll clean the two spark plugs, fill the gas tank and look for other worlds.

A Family in the Sun

When there are seven in the family, including four lively teenaged girls and their younger, even livelier brother, a few extras are hardly noticed. It's simply a matter of another potato or two in the pot, doubling up in bed or converting sofas as required. Recently, however, in a rented house in the sun-drenched Florida Keys some 2,000 miles from home, where I had to shovel two feet of snow out of the driveway before we could head south, I was dumbfounded one day to realize that my "family" had extended to more than 20. And counting.

It dawned on me early one morning when I got up to go to the kitchen for a coffee and at the end of the hallway passed by a pretty blonde young woman I had never seen before. I turned to make sure. "Would you care for a cup of coffee?" I asked.

"Love one," she replied.

"I'm Ronald Sutherland and I . . . uh . . . live here," I muttered as I poured two cups from the pot set with a timer the previous night, and we sat down at my kitchen table.

"Yes, I know," she said.

"I'm trying to place you," I muttered on. "You'll have to excuse me. I seem to be getting more and more absent-minded. Must be the sun."

"Oh, I'm Laura," she said. "You probably know my father back in Sherbrooke. I'm a friend of two of your daughters and Sharon and Angie and Bridget and Gizelle. I just drove down."

"Ah," I stated philosophically.

"Isn't this weather super?"

247

"Yes. Super. Warm too."

Then my son Colin and his friends André and Christian, who had, I think, been sleeping on camp beds in the screened porch called a Florida room, came in for breakfast, soon to be followed by my three nieces on my wife's side, Kelly, Kim and Jill.

The girls were soon in their bikinis and were taking the boat to go water-skiing. I don't know what the boys were up to. My wife and her brother and his wife and my sister were going deep-sea fishing on a charter boat, leaving my brother-in-law Keith and me to plan our attack on a huge lobster we had spotted while snorkelling the day before.

Getting that lobster was, I should point out, more than just a game. How my daughters Kate, Velma and Winona remain slim is a mystery to me. Must be the dancing they do night after night. And the boys—I won't even try to describe what teenaged boys can put away at a meal, except to say that once after a veritable mountain of fried chicken and mashed potatoes, they went out and had a Burger King whopper as a sort of digestive, followed a half-hour later by a large pizza all dressed.

Equipped with a net and a stick, Keith and I snorkelled over to the rocks where we had seen the lobster and sure enough, there it was—two feet long at least, antennas as thick as thumbs. We glided in slowly, then Keith moved to the right and poked the creature from behind. It shot forward, right into the net. But I couldn't lift the net out of the water fast enough, and the lobster hurtled out. I dove underwater, and miraculously I managed to get the net over it on the ocean bottom in about four feet of water. Keith planted both feet on the rim of the net as I came up for air.

"We've got it!" he shouted. "By God, we did it. I can feel it jumping around in the net. Go down and grab it." His back was turned, so he did not see the woman standing on the shore about six feet from us. "Quick. Go down and grab the son of a . . ."

Then Keith noticed me pointing with my finger.

"I hope you're not after my lobsters," the woman announced in an authoritative voice.

I wanted to say, "What the hell do you mean, your lobsters? This is the open sea." But I was out of breath. Keith just stood there looking bewildered. The woman then went on to explain that actually they weren't her lobsters because they were in the sea, but she liked to think of them as her own. It was all quite touching.

"Anyway," she concluded, "I can see that you two are no great threat."

And she was right. When I dove down after the delay, the giant lobster had worked its way under the rim of the net and was long gone.

Now that the holidays are over, most of the people in my extended family are gone too, back to the frozen north, and finally I have the peace and isolation I came here for. But I must say that life is now a little dull. Apart from the odd scorpion lurking at the edge of the floor mats, walking down the hallway is a lonely routine. And as I sit at my desk, I find that it is really too quiet to work properly.

Holes in the Sea

There is an old saying in the Florida Keys, known as the sport-fishing capital of the world, that a boat is "a hole in the sea surrounded by wood into which you pour money." But when I first came to this string of islands stretching from the southern tip of the mainland across the Caribbean to Key West, I was more interested in stories of hundreds of gold-laden Spanish galleons which had been wrecked along the outlying coral reef.

With the sands constantly shifting over the ocean floor, one could be scuba diving or snorkelling and suddenly come across a stack of pieces of eight. It happens all the time. The sea takes, but the sea gives back. And to explore the sea, a boat is necessary.

I knew little about boats. I knew even less about horses when I offered to go riding on Mount Royal with a gorgeous girl from Alberta many years ago. Nothing to it, I thought, having seen my share of cowboy movies. How was I to know that the riding stable would stick me with the meanest beast on the lot?

At least boats do not have minds of their own, and they do not rear up and throw innocent people six feet into the air, I told myself when I and two of my daughters stepped into the 12-foot blue boat with an ancient 18 HP Johnson outboard motor. It was my first boat, purchased for $250, and the night was falling as we pushed off from shore about a mile from where we were staying.

"We'll just whip out a couple of hundred yards and follow the coastline until we see our house," I told the girls. "Squeeze that little rubber ball to get the gas going."

"Can I drive?" asked my oldest daughter, Janet.

"Better let me," I replied. "I'll teach you both how to handle it tomorrow. You know how quickly it gets dark around here, so I'll just take us straight home."

"Yeah, and the sharks hunt at night," my other daughter added. She's the one who's always thinking of cheerful things to say.

On the third pull of the cord the motor started and away we went, all three of us staring excitedly at the foaming wake. Two, three, maybe four hundred yards from shore I veered to the right, and suddenly we heard a sickening clunk. The boat shuddered and the motor stopped.

We drifted as I tried to start the motor again, hearing ominous splashes from all sides. After about 20 minutes or so of desperately yanking at the cord, I succeeded, but the boat did not move. For some reason power was not getting to the propeller, and it was now pitch dark.

By paddling with our hands, dipping them into the water then jerking them out again, surprised each time that the hand was still there, my two daughters and I finally brought the boat back to shore. The following morning I learned about shear pins for propellers, shoals and channel markers. In the next few weeks I learned the cost of spark plugs, ignition wires, life jackets, anchors, flare guns, fire extinguishers, marine paint and bilge pumps, not to mention oil and gasoline.

Then at the end of that sojourn in the Keys, I couldn't sell the boat and was obliged to leave it with the man who had sold it to me. He solemnly promised to sell it and send me the money, but I never heard from him again.

The next time I came for an extended visit to the Florida Keys, I was naturally determined to have nothing to do with boats. But outnumbered five to one by four daughters and a son, all explaining to me that it was stupid and ridiculous to be beside the sea without a boat, I eventually gave in and bought a fibreglass model with a 35 HP motor. It had an electric starter and it worked perfectly, except that it would not go into reverse. My finances went into reverse, however, when I had to sell the boat for about $450 less than I had invested in it.

Once more living in the Florida Keys, I found myself owner of yet a third boat, equipped with a 40 HP motor and a windshield. We regularly went out in it in the evenings to witness the spectacular sunsets— the primary reason why I and so many others head south in the winter—the sun becomes a glowing red ball hovering over the horizon. Then it drops with amazing speed, and if the conditions are right it produces an emerald flash over the surface of the water the instant before it disappears.

One might almost imagine that the sun, like the fortunes spent on boats, was sinking into a hole in the sea.

Sunset of the Dolphins

The television networks and movie makers succeed quite well from tine to time. Nuclear scientists do even better. But as the devastating ice storm, the tornadoes of last summer or the volcanic eruption of Mount St. Helens clearly illustrate, even if the human race is gaining fast, nature still has the edge when it comes to spectacular performances.

Even more awesome perhaps are the memorable events which people experience unexpectedly, privately, as if nature were momentarily lifting the veil for a chosen individual. I vividly recall, for instance, the night when I was driving home over a country road in the Eastern Townships. There was a chill in the air, and it was heavy with the musky smell of fallen leaves. I slowed down when I reached the crest of a hill because I knew that the road was about to curve sharply, and as my headlights lowered, I jammed on the brakes. There, not more than ten feet in front of the car, was a magnificent stag. He was absolutely motionless, his antlers towering above his head, his eyes gleaming in the beam of light.

I too became motionless, mesmerized by the majesty of the huge creature. I reached down and turned off the motor, then I pressed in the light switch. As my eyes adjusted, I could still see the stag, standing in the moonlight now, and I'm sure that he could see me. After a few more seconds, the stag's head turned, and in one mighty bound he cleared the roadside ditch and fence and then disappeared into the woods. It was several minutes before I started up the car again and continued on home.

The only remotely similar experience I had ever had previously was an encounter with a dock rat when I was a young boy. I was going up the stairway in the wooden shed behind our flat in the East End of Montreal and the ugly rodent was coming down. There was a moment of hesitation, then the rat bared its fangs and kept coming, and I bolted out the shed door. No feeling of having had a glimpse of another world that time. Rats were all too familiar.

Another magic moment was when I got up at dawn one morning while I was living in Calgary, Alberta, looked out the window and actually saw a chinook. An arched roof of heavy grey clouds extended across the plains to the distant mountains, creating a long tunnel which appeared to lead to some luminous promised land.

But none of these experiences was quite as spellbinding as the sunset of the dolphins. My son and I were cruising in our small boat off the Florida Keys, watching the last fingers of sunlight reach up over the curved horizon and tickle the underside of blushing clouds. Then suddenly we were surrounded by a whole school of dolphins. Turning our heads from side to side we saw dozens of the sea mammals leaping three feet out of the water in graceful arcs.

These dolphins, or porpoises as they are alternatively called, were obviously examining us. I thought I could detect a glint of mirth in their eyes. They were fearless, exuberant, beautiful, and apparently trying to transmit some message to us.

My son and I now know why dolphins have fascinated people from ancient times. Modern research has determined that they have larger brains than human beings and that the elaborate series of sounds they emit among themselves may be a language of some sort, which makes them all the more fascinating. Scientists using various electronic devices are moving closer to actual communication with the dolphins. One day it could happen, and for the first time in human history the barrier between species will be broken, permitting man to move a great deal closer to harmony with nature.

That day, of course, will have to come before the nuclear scientists and military machines combine to outdo nature and produce the ultimate spectacular display. Meanwhile, the moments of magic and mystery still happen.

During the sunset of the dolphins, my son and I sat speechless as they passed by, then we increased our speed and circled around, trying to locate them again. But it was no use—they had vanished into the vastness of the sea.

"Don't worry, Dad," said my son, "we'll see them again.

I sincerely hope that he's right.

Odds and Ends

Spring Cleaning

My neighbours are all busy with their spring cleaning, and in order not to appear out of step and a lazy slob, I too have begun to get rid of a few of my tarnished treasures, otherwise known as junk.

Actually, something had to be done. The two places where I've been storing items not in use over the years, the attic and underneath the front veranda, had become as packed and impenetrable as a mangrove swamp. But a heart-rending job it is. I found the upright lamp which was a wedding gift from my fellow bandsmen in the RCAF 27 years ago. They were quite common in those days—upright lamps with elaborate shades and an entourage of little side bulbs. It had to go into storage when the kids kept knocking it over and splattering broken glass on the living-room floor.

Then I came across the old electric dryer. I had kept that going through five campaigns of proper, cloth diapers. None of these disposable paper things that are cluttering up the garbage cans and clogging the sewer systems of the Western World. Eventually I had to bypass all the controls, installing a toggle switch to turn it on and off. But it never let us down, even when I used to take out the motor periodically to operate a conveyor belt I was using while I dug out my basement.

I was startled by the number of old Chianti bottles lying about. I never could bring myself to throw away those bottles with the straw casings. They'll be worth something one of these days, I'm sure. At a flea market in Florida I once saw empty Canadian beer cans at $2 apiece.

Of all things, the old Zenith television set was still there. I bought that for $40 in a used-furniture store in Detroit and brought it home in a taxi just in time to see the famous Archie Moore/Yvon Durelle boxing match. The tubes look to be still in good shape.

My first electric lawn mower, I have to admit, has seen better days. When I tried to move it, the handle broke away from the rest of the rust-eaten machine. Still, the wheels are all right, and even though the motor is held together with haywire, it would probably run.

Strange how odd pieces of wood can bring back memories. I recognized immediately the remnants of broom handles, two-by-fours and plywood which I used to build a cradle for my daughter Katherine, who is now 35 years old and has two daughters of her own. My wife could actually rock our tiny black-haired beauty with a piece of string tied to her toe without getting out of bed.

She rocked three more of ours in the same cradle, then it was lent out to various relatives and friends. The last time it was used was for my grandson, Zachariah, and obviously it is going to be needed again in the coming few years.

That's the trouble with spring cleaning—there are so many things which simply can't be discarded. I did manage to part with the lawn mower, but only after I had spent an hour or so dismantling it. The wheels, blade and motor are bound to come in handy one of these days.

The rest of the time I spent taking apart the venerable clothes dryer. I have all the pieces except the shell in a box. If I never find use again for the motor, which dealt effectively with all those thousands of dirty diapers and tons of dirt from the basement, then I seriously think I'll have it bronzed and keep it on the mantelpiece.

At one time, as I recall, it used to be fashionable to have baby shoes bronzed. But I couldn't find any baby shoes. In the course of passing down through a string of five children they seem to have met with terminal disintegration. So I'll have to settle for the dryer motor, which in any case is probably more appropriate.

And the old wedding-gift lamp? How can I throw away something which softly lit up those long-ago evenings of loving togetherness and youthful exuberance, then miraculously survived the resulting five kids?

The rest of the spring cleaning will have to wait until next year, I'm afraid, or perhaps even longer. It is too much like dismembering oneself. And what is worse, it seems to me, is that more often than not it is like chopping off the best parts of oneself.

The Door into Summer

While I shiver in my attic study, the cold wind, having worked itself into a frenzy as it swept unimpeded across the open expanse of Lake Massawippi, is wrenching the last faded leaves from the maple tree in front of the house and rattling the window pane against the frame in a demonic attempt to get at me.

My thoughts unavoidably turn to blizzards, icy roads, freezing rain, bone-chilling gales, sleet and slush, not to mention heating bills soaring to the stars or the even bleaker prospect of supplies of furnace oil running out entirely. Once again it is time to reassure myself that there must be something good about the winter, and my old black tomcat is not providing any help. He has started the routine of meowing to go out one door. When the door is opened, he advances a few cautious steps, hesitates, turns his head with a soundless snarl, then comes back into the house and immediately begins meowing at another door.

My grandmother used to say that when a cat puts on that act it is looking for the door into summer. Incurable romantics, cats, unwilling to accept the basic crudities of life.

Mind you, many human beings in Canada and the northern states of the U.S. do much the same thing, and with a nudge or two from the travel agencies they actually find the door into summer—at the end of a carpeted ramp hooked up to the side of a sunflight jet liner, calypso music playing softly in the background.

That's one way to cope with winter, but it hardly provides the reassurance that the season as it is experienced in the North has anything to recommend it. I have observed, however, that winter does tend to produce decisiveness. People who might dilly-dally for hours over what shirt or dress to wear to a summer party will not take a moment to decide to put on their woollies when the arctic blasts are at the keyhole. This hibernal decisiveness is everywhere evident. The putty is falling out of the double windows, but they get slapped on anyway. Despite the threats that Bell will be obliged to discontinue service, without hesitation the money for the phone bill is used to buy anti-freeze for the car.

As a beekeeper, I have occasion each year to witness one of the most striking examples of how winter promotes the taking of firm decisions, and for anyone who is not a foaming-at-the-mouth feminist, a sorry business it is to behold.

The queen and the workers in a bee hive, as is well known, are female, while the drones are male. The primary function of the drones is to fertilize the queen, and quite spectacularly it must be admitted, for the union is accomplished high in the sky in full flight.

But it takes only one drone—whether the fastest, the sneakiest, the luckiest, or simply one with a flair for aerial acrobatics is not really known—to do the job, and it has to be done only once, in the spring of the year, to put the queen into a state of perpetual pregnancy. The particular drone involved kills himself in the process, having deposited not only his seed but all his reproductive equipment in her majesty. Thereafter the remaining drones merely hang around the hive, eating, sleeping and buzzing, while the females literally work themselves to death.

With the brisk autumn breezes and the shrivelled blossoms, however, comes the awful day of reckoning. In preparation for the exigencies of winter, the drones are dragged out of the hive and left to expire on the frosty ground.

Often have I watched, helpless to intervene, as three or four heartless females intercepted a drone trying to crawl unobtrusively back into the hive. His chances are nil. Bees operate by the absolute rule of maximum efficiency. The greater good of the collectivity must prevail. Drones would do nothing but take up space and deplete the winter stores of pollen and honey, so they have to go.

Winter, thus, does have beneficial effects—it fosters the character-building qualities of practicality and decisiveness. Which explains why Canada, half the year at least and with the possible exception of relatively mild Victoria, B.C., is a nation of resolute, strong-willed, unwavering people with the capacity to make quick and pragmatic decisions.

I myself stand as a shining example. The wind is still rattling my window pane trying to get at me, and this very minute I have made the firm decision to call my travel agent and book passage through the door into summer.

Jack Daniels

Few may yet have noticed, but the Société des Alcools du Québec, which tourists have been known to refer to as the Quebec Alcoholics' Society, is now stocking Jack Daniels Tennessee Whisky, and this gives rise, however inappropriately, to sobering thoughts.

Jack Daniels, you see, is not just your ordinary still-on-the-hill corn liquor, although undoubtedly that's how it started. These days, in fact, it is widely esteemed as the Cadillac, the Concorde supersonic jet, the royal suite at the Ritz of sour-mash bourbon whiskies. There is, to be sure, a hint of the sinister about it. Lynchburg is the infelicitous name of the town where it is distilled, and in 1915, of all things, it was awarded a certificate of the London Institute of Hygiene.

Lynchburg, moreover, is in a dry county, I'm told, which means that the people who make Jack Daniels cannot legally drink the stuff themselves. Mind you, if there's any truth to the tales about the buzzards in the sky becoming so drunk they can't fly, then the distillery workers don't have to drink it. All they have to do is breathe it. Besides, there's always a leak or two in every dry county.

Not too long ago I was staying with my wife's family in the hills of Kentucky about five miles from the Tennesee border. While the county I was in had total prohibition of booze, the adjoining county on the Tennessee side was wide open. It varies from county to county.

The roads in this mountainous area are incredibly narrow and twisty. Locals joked that it was the only place in the world where driving fast at night you could see your own tail lights. Trying to make conversation with an old man in a store one day—and it isn't easy, because these hill people don't trust strangers—I repeated one of my father-in-law's stories about how one particularly contorted road had been laid out by a surveyor tying a log to the tail of a mule and letting the animal wander home. The surveyor and the mule were from a dry county, and the road started in a wet county, where the man had gotten too drunk to do his job properly. The old man eyed me suspiciously, obviously confused that an outsider with a strange accent should have garnered such inside lore. But he was not to be outdone.

"Thet thar mule," he finally remarked, "musta bin followin' a snake."

Bootleggers, of course, flourish in dry counties. I had occasion to visit one when my wife's uncle Ray decided that he wanted a nip of white lightning to celebrate his birthday.

"Jest round the bend," Ray kept assuring me as we drove miles up a corkscrew dirt lane. The dogwood, something like a huge apple blossom, and the gorgeous, flaming redbud were in bloom, but I couldn't look. The road was one continuous bend. Finally we reached Eb's shack, and I realized that cartoonist Al Capp had not been nearly as inventive as I used to think. Five hound dogs basked motionless in the sun. A cocked shotgun leaned against the railing of the tiny veranda beside the old rocker where Eb sat chewing tobacco. I knew when he narrowed his eyes at me and then noted the outlandish Quebec licence plates with words in some foreign language that Ray was not going to have an easy time of it.

"Mighty hot, Eb," said Ray.

"Yep, mighty hot," replied Eb.

"Mighty dry, Eb," ventured Ray.

"Yep, mighty dry," said Eb. Then he spit over the railing.

We stood waiting. I tried to make myself as inconspicuous as possible. Finally Eb spoke, looking pointedly at me. "Reckon it's aimin' to stay dry," he said.

We got back into the car and threaded our spiritless way home. No doubt the original Mr. Jack Daniels was much like Eb, but somewhere along the line the product acquired a special mystique. I am informed by a fairly reliable source, who will remain nameless for the sake of marital continuity, that traditionally there are four kinds of Kentucky and Tennesee hooches: drinkin' whisky, fightin' whisky, courtin' whisky and sippin' whisky. Now Jack Daniels apparently has not been definitively placed in any one of these categories, but we do know that it has become closely associated with the Petroleum Industry. Where the oil men go, Jack is sure to follow—Texas, Alberta, Venezuela and even, outrage of outrages, the land of the magic malt, Scotland.

Quebec, however, as we are all chillingly aware, does not produce a drop of crude oil. How then has the Lynchburg lotion come down from the hills to be found on our shelves between the MacNish and Vat 69? The explanation, I suspect, is that Jack Daniels is really a wishin' whisky. And God knows, in these troubled times, we need all the good wishes we can get. Cheers!

Peerless Juries

The man who got to keep the mule is what immediately comes to my mind when I think about trials by jury. The right to be tried by a jury of one's peers is, of course, a basic principle of the systems of justice throughout North America and in other parts of the civilized world, but like democracy itself, it doesn't always work as smoothly as it should.

A recent, much publicized trial of six men for the gang rape of a woman on a bar-room pool table provides a bizarre example. Before the trial, some 3,000 people held a candlelight parade in support of the victim, demanding that the culprits be punished with the full force of the law. But as soon as the jury found four of the accused guilty of aggravated rape, 10,000 people marched through the streets claiming a miscarriage of justice.

Now presumably the six men and six women in the jury of peers were of the persuasion of the first 3,000 demonstrators, but what if the majority of them had been like-minded to the second 10,000? The verdict might have been the reverse. In other words, perhaps the whole trial could have been as fairly resolved by flipping a coin.

The problem seems to lie in the word "peer," which by dictionary definition is "an equal, as in natural gifts or in social rank." Is it really possible to form a jury of one's peers, and is it necessarily a good thing to attempt to do at all?

Many years ago in the Eastern Townships of Quebec, there was a murder trial which is still talked about when the old folks gather around the fireplace.

It seems that a much-respected man in a small town married a city girl, who turned out to be a Jezebel and a Salome rolled into one nasty lady. She made the poor man's life pure hell, stealing from him, cheating on him and abusing him in ever more diabolical ways. One night when she staggered in the door, he shot her. His attempt also to shoot himself resulted only in a superficial head wound.

A jury of the man's peers was formed and the trial began. Witnesses were called who testified explicitly to the murdered woman's bad character. Other witnesses swore that they had seen a sinister-looking stranger in town the day of the crime and that the accused had the habit of taking long walks at night when he couldn't sleep worrying about his wife. The defendant himself pleaded total amnesia as a result of his head injury. Apparently the jury did not even need to deliberate to come to the verdict of not guilty. And that was the end of that. The local man had literally gotten away with murder.

Even more remarkable was the decision of a jury in the hills of rural Kentucky. The event was described to me by my father-in-law, Luther Carter, who claimed to have attended the trial. Before radio and television, he said, trials were the major form of entertainment in those parts.

The accused was a dirt-farmer, a man who barely scraped a living from the rocky soil in the hills, getting by with a few chickens and hogs and a small crop of tobacco, like most of his neighbours. One local and highly unpopular man, however, had a large estate on the fertile flat land bordering a river. The accused had been caught with a mule bearing the estate's brand.

When the circuit judge came around, the farmer who had stolen the mule opted for a trial by a jury of his peers, and a dozen other dirt-farmers in the area were summoned for duty. The sheriff, naturally, testified to the brand on the animal as irrefutable evidence. The jury then retired for two or three hours to chew tobacco and ponder the evidence. When they returned to the courtroom, the judge asked the foreman if they had reached a decision.

"Yes, judge. We find the defendant not guilty, provided he returns the mule."

The judge was apparently infuriated. He pointed out that the decision was ridiculous, a total contradiction. If the defendant was expected to return the damned mule, then obviously he had stolen it in the first place, and that was what the trial was all about. The judge then ordered the members of the jury to retire again and to come back with a decision making a little more sense.

Well, out they went to chew and ponder for another couple of hours, according to my father-in-law, and when they returned, the judge once again asked the foreman if the jury had arrived at a verdict.

"Yes, judge," the foreman replied.

"And what is your verdict?" asked the judge.

"We find the defendant not guilty, and he can keep the mule."

Trial by a jury of so-called peers, thus, can be a highly dubious means to achieve justice. But aside from the even more doubtful option of a lone judge, what else can we do? Unless a genius finds a way to program an electronic brain with the wisdom of Solomon, or else by some miracle women and men learn to treat each other properly, and our society develops a better distribution of mules.

Comets and Mortality

During his last few years, my father-in-law, Luther Carter, had one fervent wish: he wanted to see Halley's Comet, which appears every 76 years and was due at the end of 1986. Moreover, he wanted to see it with his only great-grandson and my grandson, Zachariah.

The reason for this wish was that he had witnessed the previous visit of Halley's Comet in 1910 in the company of a great-aunt who had herself seen the earlier appearance of the comet in the 1830s. But Mr. Carter's wish was not to be fulfilled. He died a few months before the arrival of the comet. And just a few days before, another close family member, my Uncle Bob Goudie, also died, giving me the unpleasant duty of attending two funerals in three weeks.

Neither death was tragic or untimely. Uncle Bob was in fact nearly 88 years old and exceeded what might well have been his life expectancy by some 68 years. As a youth in the Canadian Army during World War I he had been a victim of a poison gas attack. Not yet 20 years old, he was sent home a complete wreck—shell-shocked, emaciated, no hair on his head and lungs not expected to last more than a few weeks.

But somehow he survived. He used to go out west with the harvest crews and apparently the tough physical labour, fresh air and wholesome food helped him to regain his strength. He also had the good fortune of marrying a solid French-Canadian girl from Trois-Rivières, who took good care of him, and of all the rest of the family when we got together over the years. I suspect that wives often have a greater effect

271

on their husbands' life expectancy than medical science or living habits.

My father-in-law was in his 85th year, and he too had lived a full and seemingly charmed life. Born in the hills of Kentucky, he had served as a young man in the U.S. Marines, at one time as part of the occupation force in the Dominican Republic, where the rebels were no more appreciative of Yankee intervention than many contemporary nationals.

He then became a policeman in Detroit during Prohibition, when the gangsters and bootleggers in the motor city were making the Dominican Republic seem like a quiet vacation spot in the Caribbean sunshine. The Great Depression years saw Mr. Carter back on the old dirt farm in Kentucky, trying to eke out a living with a few hogs and crops of corn and tobacco.

Eventually he returned to Michigan, where he worked into his seventies as a male nurse in the famous Ypsilanti Asylum for the insane. He was there when one of the institution's psychiatrists conducted the experiment with three men all claiming to be Jesus Christ which was subsequently described in the book *The Three Christs of Ypsilanti*. The three men were kept together over a period of time to determine how they would react to one another, presumably in the hope that two would relinquish the claim to divinity. I can't recall exactly how the experiment worked out, and my father-in-law is no longer around to refresh my memory. He had an extraordinary memory himself, was a born raconteur and had a marvellous sense of humour and irony.

At one time on a sabbatical leave I rented a house on the Florida Keys which turned out to be in a community almost exclusively of millionaires. Before long, solely by virtue of being there, I was receiving regular invitations to the daily afternoon cocktail parties. When my father-in-law came to visit, he came with me to one, and I introduced him as Mr. Carter from Kentucky.

"Ah, race horses," immediately responded one of the well-heeled assembly.

"Well, . . . no," quietly replied my rather distinguished-looking father-in-law as three or four other guests turned towards us, "just a few hogs and a little tobacco."

Now I knew that Mr. Carter had never made more than $500 in a good year on the rocky dirt farm, but I swear that I could visualize the vast numbers of piggeries and endless rolling fields of tobacco somehow being conjured up in the minds of the people gathered around us at that cocktail party. After all, we were there, weren't we?

"Of course, of course," said the first man. "Much more reliable than the horses."

Then he turned to another man a few feet away. "Hey, Len," he called out, "come over here and meet Mr. Carter from Kentucky. He's in hogs and tobacco."

An hour or so later, as the sun set over the Gulf of Mexico, my father-in-law and his new millionaire buddies were still in deep consultation while sipping mint juleps under the palm trees. It's been a trying period for me, these last few months. First my close friend from childhood, Elinor Lewis, died tragically and prematurely after a long bout with cancer, then my old friend the poet and lawyer Frank Scott, then my uncle and my father-in-law.

Like Mr. Carter, Frank Scott had a wish. Born in 1899, he used to say that he wanted to see three centuries. Well, that was not to be either. Perhaps, however, all four of the people I lost saw Halley's Comet from a closer proximity than the rest of us mortals.

A Country for Giants

Now that the grass is green again and the exuberant tulips among various other delicate blossoms are celebrating the defeat of winter, I have put the lawn furniture back on the patio, and I couldn't help noticing that the aging chairs are becoming a bit delicate too.

I worry about the sturdiness of chairs. A few years ago, my brother-in-law Keith, about 230 pounds at the time, was over for a barbecue, and we were sitting across from each other at the table. As we ate and talked, I had the impression that he was moving sideways and sinking, but I dismissed it as an illusion caused by the ever-treacherous combination of hot sun and cold beer. Then suddenly he disappeared altogether. The metal-and-canvas chair had simply folded at the joints and collapsed, leaving him sprawled on the grass.

My brother-in-law is actually petite compared with others I have known. As a youth in the East End of Montreal I used to go out with a pretty girl called Joan. She was a shapely normal size, but she had four older brothers, one of whom was six foot six, about 300 pounds and an ex-commando. Big Lloyd Welcher could open coke bottles with a flick of his thumb, and I'll never forget the Saturday afternoon he invited me out to a tavern while his wife and Joan were busy sewing or something of the sort.

The tavern was full of beefy stevedores, and in the East End we knew that meant trouble. When they saw the challenge of Lloyd walk in, their eyes lit up like pinball machines, something which did not escape the waiter's notice. "I'm sorry, the boss says I can't serve you," he announced half-pleadingly, his eyes anxiously shifting back and forth between our table and the gang of attentive longshoremen.

"I brought my friend here for a beer, so you just get it the hell over here," said Lloyd in a loud voice. He, naturally, was immune to intimidation. I grabbed a chair and backed into a corner as I saw the room come alive.

Bodies literally flew through the air. One mighty kick felled three men at the same time. When it was all over five minutes later, at least a dozen stevedores were on the floor, and the others had disappeared. Lloyd then calmly sat back down as if he had just returned from the washroom. I returned from the corner with my chair, and the waiter, stepping around bodies on the floor, rushed over with two beers.

I have described elsewhere the big strike which took place at the Canadian Vickers firm in the East End and how Lloyd, my brother-in-law, and others were involved. I happened to be at Joan's place when Lloyd phoned to say that his friend Tiny would soon be arriving. When the doorbell rang and I went to the door, I could see nobody through the glass and was about to turn away when the bell rang again. I opened the door to meet Tiny, who actually had to bend down in order to enter the house.

More recently, when the movie *Suzanne* was being made from one of my novels, I worked with another colossus, director Robin Spry, who stands six foot four and has not weighed himself for many years because standard scales only go up to 300 pounds.

Robin has conditioned himself to walk on floors and to sit cautiously, particularly since attending a party at an elegant country chalet. He and the others were dancing on the wide veranda, under a roof supported by corner posts. As the party progressed, someone started a conga line, and the whole group began to snake around the veranda. The leader then grabbed one of the corner posts, swung out over the lawn and parking lot, then back onto the veranda again. The others in the line followed suit, including Robin Spry. Only in his case, he didn't swing back. The post he was gripping separated from the roof, and he landed on top of his host's new Cadillac at the same time as the roof began to buckle.

I know many other big people—Edgar Stracchino, who weighed 312 pounds in his prime; John Lennox, who towers to six feet eight inches; as well as my old friend and colleague of many years Gerry Cappon and historian Mason Wade, neither of whom has to lift his head far to look John in the eye. My nephew Bruce Wilkins, a former pro football player, and his brother Barry, a policeman in Calgary, are both closer to 300 than 200 pounds, and my own husky son, whom I used to cradle in one arm, is moving in that direction, as are his buddies Chris Enright and Ian Matthews. Several local Eastern Townships men qualify as legitimate heavyweights, including master carpenter Bob Ditchburn and Greg Bishop, who is now an RCMP officer.

Come to think of it, in fact, maybe Quebec poet Jean-Guy Pilon was close to the truth when he wrote about Canada: "There are countries for children, and others for men . . . some few only for giants. . . ." Now if only the people who manufacture lawn furniture could be persuaded to read more poetry.

Quebec Bugs

The province of Quebec, according to a recently published statement by University of Toronto entomologist Susan McIntyre, has the highest density of bugs in the world, "including the tropics."

As someone who has co-existed with the creatures of Quebec all my life, I find this information mind-boggling. I start to itch just thinking about it. Surely having the highest density of taxes is enough for one province. The woman has to be making some mistake.

Once, for instance, I rented a room in downtown Detroit. It looked clean and proper enough in the afternoon, but when I returned late in the evening and turned on the lights, I actually thought that the walls were moving. Then I realized that they were covered with platoons of cockroaches scurrying in all directions.

"Ya shoulda bin here the year of the giant flying roaches," chuckled the landlady when I went to complain. "An inch an' a half long they was, an' two of 'em together could haul off a medium-sized pizza. Come in on a loada bananas or somethin'. Pretty soon there was millions an' millions of 'em."

"My God!" I exclaimed. "What did you do?"

"Couldn't do nothin'. If ya tried to get near 'em, they just took off like little rockets. They had these wings, you see. Now them was cockroaches, let me tell ya."

"What happened to them?"

"Disappeared with the cold weather, just like most of the politicians around here. Flew back to where they come from, I reckon."

There seemed to be no point in continuing the discussion. Wishing that I could fly back to where I had come from, spic-and-span, pristine-and-pure Montreal, I went to the corner store and bought a case of Raid.

I admit that we used to see the odd cockroach in the flat on Adam Street in the East End where I grew up, but such a sighting always sent my Aunt Janet, who was a fanatic about cleanliness in any case, into a virtual housekeeping frenzy. Our kitchen table was regularly scrubbed with so much vigour that it came to resemble a half moon, and I used to have to stack up the mashed potatoes at the top rim of my plate to keep the peas from rolling off.

I have been to many places in the world which must have been more insect-infested than my native Quebec. The termites in Georgia could devour the floor beams of a house while the owner nipped out for a happy hour, and the black flies in northern Ontario could devour an owner while he was installing a floor beam.

I've seen ants in the Bahamas clean the conch out of a huge conch shell in less than the time between strikes in Montreal, and in the swamplands of South Carolina I've watched fogs of mosquitoes dim the light of a full moon.

At the remarkable May's Insect Museum near Colorado Springs, my son and I, possibly the only two people who have visited the place in years, saw specimens of all the insects of the American Southwest, including rhinoceros beetles about the size of Volkswagens and preserved tarantulas enjoying an everlasting feast of stuffed humming-birds.

Which all makes me wonder. Who is this Susan McIntyre anyway? When it comes to pronounce-ments on Quebec, can people from Ontario, especially scientists from the University of Toronto, if indeed there really is a university in Toronto, be trusted? How exactly did this woman get so familiar with our bugs? I mean what sort of places does she hang out at when she comes to Quebec?

If by some chance Ms McIntyre does know what she's talking about, then the only explanation I can think of is that it's all the fault of one-time premier René Lévesque. Apparently insects themselves are the most effective means of controlling the popula-tions of other insects, much like human beings. Spiders eat flies of course, praying mantises take time out from their supplications to chomp up hapless grasshoppers clutched in their grotesque front legs, and scorpions—especially scorpions—cut a wide swath through the ranks of their co-arthropods. Now one of the top bug-men in Quebec was René Lévesque himself. His famous observation about the relationship between Quebec and English Canada, as I've mentioned before, was that they are "two scor-pions in a bottle."

As everyone knows, scorpions are rare in Quebec. In fact, René's two may be the only ones we've got. And it occurs to me that if somehow his nationalist followers could see fit to let them out of the bottle, we would go a long way towards solving the problem of the bugs in *la belle province*, not to mention the rest of the country.

Summer Jobs

My five children—it's a bit unnerving to consider that they now range in age from 18 to 24—are all looking for suitable summer jobs, and I gather that with hundreds of thousands of regular wage-earners out of work, the opportunities are few these days.

Back in the 1950s, when I was working my way through college, I never had any trouble finding summer jobs. Of course, I was not quite as sophisticated as young people today, who bandy about such terms as personality enhancement, career compatibility and self-realization. I don't know where they get all these notions. I was willing to do just about anything short of contracts with Murder Inc. to put a few dollars in my pocket, and often enough summer jobs turned out to be more educational than the courses I took during the academic year.

My first summer job was as a bus boy for the old Blue Cake Counter in Eaton's department store. The highlight of that stint, aside from the time when a disgruntled baker cut the throat of a dietician, was when two fellow bus boys dropped a wedding cake. It was no ordinary cake. Two or three pastry experts had worked on it for days, building up the several tiers, applying the icing in elaborate designs, adding little flowers, the bride-and-groom figurines, the requested lettering. Then an hour or so before the wedding, the cake had to be placed in a large cardboard container for delivery.

Most of the employees were standing around admiring the creation when it hit the floor, to be instantly transformed into a heap of pastry mush. I hope the marriage lasted a little longer.

Another summer at Eaton's I worked as a clerk in the women's shoe department. It was trying at times, waiting patiently as some perverse old doll who took size nine insisted on testing every size eight in the stockroom, but the tedium was relieved by the occasional close-up display of a pair of shapely legs. Penny loafers were the craze among teenaged girls at the time, and the teenaged shoe salesman who gently slipped them onto dainty feet sometimes ended up with a date as well as a sale.

In striking contrast, I worked another summer digging ditches among a gang of sweating, snorting, cursing men. I acquired a good tan, a lot of muscle and the ability to down a quart of cold beer within five minutes of arrival at a nearby tavern after work. But about the only educational episode was when one of my fellow labourers rammed a company truck into a Coke machine which had delivered an empty bottle for his last dime.

One summer a classmate at McGill and I decided to hire out as non-union painters. Any idiot can splash paint on a wall, we both reasoned. Our first contract was a four-storey stairwell in a new garment factory. "What kind of size will you use?" the factory owner asked when we arrived at the job. Neither of us had ever heard of size, apparently a pre-coating liquid needed to seal new plaster.

"The usual kind," my partner quickly replied. But since the contract required us to supply the materials, we decided to pass on the size. We also decided that a strip of scotch tape along the lower edge of the light-coloured upper wall would allow us to have a perfectly straight line between the upper and the darker bottom half.

Needless to say, the job was a disaster. By the time we were half-way down the stairwell, the paint was already fading and rubbing off the top. When I removed the scotch tape, ragged strips of paint came with it. I rushed out and bought a water-colour brush and tried to repair the damage, but I just made it worse. With a marked lack of delicacy, the owner told us to stuff our paint brushes and get the hell out of his factory.

Later that summer my friend and I sold air conditioners, two to be exact. Then he was hospitalized with carbon-monoxide poisoning because the old Anglia we used for transportation was letting in exhaust fumes. I was spared because I smoked a pipe and kept the window open.

I was a Fuller Brush man for a while, going door to door in Point St. Charles. I soon learned that when I stepped into a flat desperately in need of a broom, the item I had the best chance of selling was egg cream shampoo. Then my last summer jobs were as a reporter for the late *Montreal Star*, where I learned to spell accommodate with two 'm's, type a five-paragraph story with two fingers in the two minutes before deadline, and even more about human nature than I had learned in my previous summer jobs. And some of it I would have rather not learned, such as the depths of depravity possible in cases of child abuse.

But the kids are probably right—employment opportunities aren't what they used to be. I guess I'm lucky to be long past having to look for a summer job. A lot of things aren't what they used to be. Including myself.

Crows, Raccoons, Crab Grass and Nuclear Dumps

"It's an ill wind that blows nobody good," my grand-mother used to say, and residents of the idyllic Eastern Townships of Quebec, a region of rolling green hills, lakes and streams, are speculating these days about the possible blessings which will come from a nearby nuclear dump.

Recently it became known that the U.S. Department of Energy is in the process of considering a number of sites in 17 states as potential repositories for radioactive waste. After all, something has to be done with the stuff. It can't be just left lying around like wrecked cars and half-moon bedsprings.

One of the proposed sites eventually to contain 70,000 metric tonnes of nuclear materials is right smack on the Quebec-Vermont border, and three others are within a distance of 20 miles. Since as far back as anyone can remember, the watershed from all four of the sites under study has flowed directly into Quebec's Lakes Memphremagog, Massawippi and Lovering and thus affects the source of drinking water for the city of Sherbrooke and numerous other towns and municipalities.

I understand, however, that the maps used by officials of the U.S. Department of Energy do not show anything north of the border, so they couldn't be expected to know what happens to the water once it has wantonly deserted the country.

But they have established stringent criteria for the selection of dump sites, it is comforting to know. The main factor—proximity to high-density populations—

in fact puts Vermont, with a mere 529,396 people the least populous of the 17 states involved, in a "favoured" position. Once again, U.S. officials could not be expected to know that hundreds of thousands of Canadians live just on the other side of the border. The Massawippi Water Protection Association and other townships' groups have been fretting a bit of late about sinister implications of nuclear dumps. They've even gone so far as to suggest that the Quebec and Canadian governments pressure the U.S. to recognize, if not the rights of Canadians, then at least their existence.

But perhaps that is asking too much. Everybody is picking on the poor Americans, and our own governments have enough to do without having to worry about the people. Besides, it is not as if we've ever had any commitment to the environment.

The carnage of porcupines, groundhogs, skunks and various other small animals on our highways, for example, is appalling. Most of the killing, I gather, takes place at night, when the creatures are stunned by headlights and simply freeze until they become tire thumps. Larger animals are killed too. Moose and deer are attracted by the salt spread on roads to melt the ice in winter. One morning I counted 16 slaughtered deer on a new interstate highway in Pennsylvania.

Construction of new roads no doubt hangs on many factors considered more important than the paths habitually followed by wandering or migrating quadrupeds. Driving up to Montreal a few days ago, however, I could not help noticing that the ill wind of highway massacre is a bonanza to at least one creature—the crow.

Their raven feathers gleaming in the dawn sunlight, the scavenger birds are so fat that they can hardly fly. Actually they have no need to do more than waddle from one mangled carcass to the next, taking to the air only now and again, quite likely to dip their wings in homage to the service stations.

The other creature North American civilization has bestowed unusual benefits upon is the raccoon, which, having adapted to a diet more or less identical to man's, is flourishing on the leftovers of a society which throws away as much as it uses. For years I have matched wits with raccoons to keep them from spreading garbage all over the road in front of my house. I once devised a three-spring latch for my metal trash can and watched in gleeful triumph as four raccoons futilely tried to unfasten it. But finally I had to build a hut for the can, because the garbage men couldn't figure out the latch either.

I have cats, and I cut out a little swinging panel in the back door to let them come and go as they please. And it worked fine . . . until the raccoons caught on, that is. I came downstairs one morning to find every square inch of the kitchen floor covered with crumbs, sugar, molasses and most of the week's groceries, and a huge raccoon peacefully asleep on the kitchen counter. As a supreme gesture of disdain, he had deposited a scented message on top of the breadbox, which he had not been able to open.

There was nothing for it—I had to board up the cats' door, and they had to meow again when they wanted in or out.

It was about two weeks later that I heard a noise at the back door, a sort of raucous meow, and I thought at first that one of the cats had a cold or had been hurt. I rushed to the door, opened it, and so help me God, there it was—the huge raccoon meowing like a cat! And to top it all off, the wretched beast walked right past me into the house, without even looking up.

But I suppose that even the wily raccoons would not be immune from an accident or an unforeseen development at a nuclear waste dump. Although I suspect that they would adapt, for a while at least.

It has been said that when the oxygen-producing rain forest of Brazil is eventually cut down, when the jet planes and various emissions have erased the ozone layer, when acid rain has killed all the fish and modern civilization has generally achieved an irreversible level of pollution, crab grass will inherit the earth.

Gasping for breath, consumed with cancer, gazing at a sunset made spectacularly luminous by enormous clouds of dust, brighter almost than the glowing piles of radioactive waste surrounding him, the last man will sink to his knees.

Watching him from the shoulder of what was once a great highway will be a fat, wingless crow. And watching the crow from a clump of six-foot-high crab grass will be a gigantic furry monster with beady eyes and a black-and-white-ringed bushy tail, lifting its head slowly to sniff the ill wind.

Kids, Cats and Jaws

It's an affront to my pride, of course, but over the years I've more or less gotten used to being identified not as myself but as the father of one of my kids— "You're Kate's old man, aren't you?" —"I know who you are, you're Colin's Dad." What is truly ego-shattering, however, is to discover that to quite a few people right in my home town I'm known only as the man who has the old yellow dog.

I never wanted a dog. In fact, when the kids came home with a scruffy little stray puppy about the size and colour of a bread roll, I gave them one hour to get rid of it. When they couldn't find a taker, under extreme pressure I extended the time limit to two hours. Twelve years have now gone by, the kids have grown up, and Hellmutt is still here.

He has been called the Massawippi Monster because he often swims far out into the lake by our house, bobbing up and down in the waves with his mouth wide open and his prominent fangs protruding. He is also known as Jaws, the result of his perverse obsession with chasing water skiers.

He watches from the lakeside road, and when he spots a skier he hurtles down the stairway to the shore, picking up speed as he rockets to the end of our dock. Then he leaps into the air and hits the water about 15 feet out, his four legs paddling so fast that he actually leaves a wake. And this technique, unfortunately, sometimes succeeds—he has caught two water skiers so far this year, and one of them threatened me with a lawsuit. What he does is clamp his jaws on a ski so that the skier is knocked off balance and tumbles into the water.

With seven different people telling him what to do, Hellmutt has never really been trained. But if old dogs can't be taught new tricks, this old dog can certainly teach himself a few. This summer, when we tried to confine him to the house and porch to avoid lawsuits, he quickly figured out how to open the porch screen door, pulling it towards himself with one paw placed at the bottom of the screen and deftly stepping through before the door closed again.

Why on earth he wants to chase water skiers, though, is a great mystery. Otherwise he is an extremely gentle, good-natured dog. We like to think that his motives are humanitarian, that he is trying to rescue someone he thinks is being abducted by a maniac in a motor boat, and we have the usual allotment of such maniacs on Lake Massawippi. He is a regal-looking mutt, always poised with his head high and his ears rigidly upright, and I often wonder what goes on in his canine mind.

Lately, however, I've had other resident creatures to ponder. We now find ourselves with 11 cats, and I have been trying to find out if it is possible to sue a veterinarian for malpractice.

My wife, a cat fancier and sentimentalist, insisted that we allow Wrong-way Corrigan (so named because we often had to turn her around and plug her in at feeding time when she was a kitten) to have one litter before being "fixed," and we managed to give away three of the five kittens, which was not too bad. Meanwhile, the vet assured us that our loose-living, sleek black pussy cat, who struts around with her tail in the air, could not get pregnant so long as she was still nursing. When she started to swell like a balloon, we presumed that she had some kind of tumour and took her back to the vet. He muttered that the case was uncommon, but that Corrigan was indeed pregnant again and would produce two kittens in about four weeks.

Three weeks later, at five o'clock in the morning, she was meowing and scratching at the side of my bed. I opened one eye and told her to go downstairs to her prepared box. When she persisted, I peeked over the side of the bed to see that she had already deposited a kitten on one of my socks.

I woke my wife and rushed downstairs myself to get the box. By the time I got back, Corrigan had dropped another kitten on my other sock. I placed socks, kittens and pussy cat into the box, carried the whole works down the stairs, then looked down to see that there were now four kittens. So much for the vet's two, I thought.

While I was having a post-natal coffee, the young son of French-speaking house guests, the Beauchesnes, happened to come in, and I told him to go look at the new-born kittens. He came back in a couple of minutes holding up five fingers and saying "*cinq.*" Kids can't even count any more, I said to myself as I took him over to the box to demonstrate his error.

Pointing to each one, I started to count—*Un, deux, trois, quatre . . . cinq? . . . cinq . . . six! . . . SEPT!!* When Corrigan had finally completed her profligate delivery, there were eight black kittens in the box.

I really don't know what we're going to do. We've already downloaded on every neighbour and acquaintance with the slightest affection for animals, and lately people have taken to avoiding me in the shops and on the street. They imagine that I don't notice them ducking behind display racks or darting up side roads.

Although I must say that it is amusing to watch the eight tiny balls of fur climbing all over the big yellow dog, who looks down at them balefully and with great disdain. Their mother used to do the same and often slept snuggled up to Hellmutt's belly. More than ever I wonder what is going on in his mind. After all, it must be quite ego-deflating for the renowned Jaws, the legendary Massawippi Monster, to be treated with such disrespect by creatures not much bigger than his paws.

And as for myself, I can already see it coming. It is just a matter of time now until I become known as the guy on the hill who has a house full of cats.

AGMV Marquis

MEMBER OF SCABRINI MEDIA

Quebec, Canada
2004